# Bright Intervals

---

40 Brief Worship Services
And Meditations
For Any Occasion

---

# Robert A. Beringer

CSS Publishing Company, Inc., Lima, Ohio

**Library of Congress Cataloging-in-Publication Data**

Beringer, Robert, 1936-
    Bright intervals : 40 brief worship services and meditations for any occasion / Robert A. Beringer.
        p.    cm.
    ISBN 0-7880-1337-8 (pbk.)
    1. Worship programs.   I. Title.
BV198.B45        1999
264—dc21                                                                        98-49322
                                                                                    CIP

This book is available in the following formats, listed by ISBN:
    0-7880-1337-8   Book
    0-7880-1338-6   Disk
    0-7880-1339-4   Sermon Prep

*In gratitude to
Peggy, David, Peter, Beth, and Tom
for all they have taught me
about the wonder of God's amazing love*

# Table Of Contents

## Services For Special Days And Seasons

# Introduction

When my family and I spent a summer in Scotland on a pulpit exchange, we became accustomed to the phrase "bright intervals" every time we listened to a weather forecast. The day's forecast was almost always something like "rain with bright intervals" or "cloudy with bright intervals."

Every life needs some bright intervals. For many persons as we grow older, it is a time of worship that provides a bright interval in the routine of our days. In worship, we experience God's presence in our lives, and are renewed both in mind and heart by singing familiar hymns of faith and hearing God's word in scripture.

This book is designed to help those who lead brief services of worship in health care centers, retirement homes, nursing homes, or hospitals. There is a total of forty services in this book; where possible, I have tried to follow the Christian Year as well as national holidays.

Each service includes a call to worship and opening prayer, the background of a favorite hymn that fits the theme of the service, a scripture reading, a meditation, and where appropriate, a closing prayer or benediction. I have found that residents of health care centers enjoy the opportunity to repeat the Lord's Prayer and Psalm 23 on a regular basis. The reader will find both humorous and inspirational stories that will enliven these short meditations.

It is my prayer that these resources will assist you in planning brief worship experiences that will bring hope and encouragement to all who share them together.

Robert A. Beringer

# 1. A Show Of Hands

**Greeting and Call To Worship**
*This is the day the Lord has made; let us rejoice and be glad in it!*

**Opening Prayer**
Creator God, we give thanks for this day which you have made. Be present with us in the power of your Holy Spirit to bless our worship and praise. In Jesus' name we pray. Amen.

**Lord's Prayer**

**Special Hymn** "Blessed Assurance"
The words to this hymn were written by Fanny Crosby, who lived from 1820 until 1915. Having lost her sight as an infant, Fanny Crosby did not begin writing hymns until she was 41 years old. Hymn writing then became her mission in life, and she wrote nearly 8,000 hymns before her death. As we sing the words, "Blessed assurance, Jesus is mine," let the words of this confident Christian woman be an inspiration to you.

**Scripture Reading** John 20:24-29

**Meditation**
One of the time-honored rituals in most families with growing children occurs when it is time for dinner. Children are called from play, and the parent says, "Now let me see your hands!" Those hands reveal sometimes more than our children even imagine — the grimy evidences of the latest construction project in the back-yard or the forbidden paint can in the garage.

But it is true of all ages. Our hands often tell a great deal about the person we are. How different are the hands of an auto mechanic from the hands of a concert pianist! We use our hands to express a variety of feelings. Often when we meet a friend, we shake hands. At a meeting people express their opinion by a show of hands.

Too often people use their hands in the wrong way. They become judgmental and point an accusing finger at someone. How interesting though that when your index finger is pointing out someone else's faults, three of your own fingers are pointing back at you! Other people use their hands to make a fist, and to hurt those who in some fashion they consider their enemies.

But in the story of Thomas, Jesus demonstrated that our hands can be used in the service of God. Jesus knew that mere words would not be enough to convince Thomas of his Resurrection. So he invited this honest questioner to touch his hands, and see for himself that the person standing before him was none other than the same Jesus who had been nailed to a cross. It was that show of hands that convinced Thomas to utter one of the most heartfelt expressions of faith ever made: "My Lord and my God!"

Think of all the ways God can use our hands in the service of Christ today. Even if our hands are gnarled by arthritis, every one of us in this room can lift our hands in prayer. Who of us has not been inspired by that famous sculpture of "The Praying Hands"? Lifting up our hands to pray for ourselves, our families, our neighbors, and our world is something every Christian can do.

Some of you are in a position to lend a hand to those around you who need a little help. We must never forget how even the tiniest gesture of love can communicate the love of Jesus to those around us. Remember Jesus saying, "Inasmuch as you have done it unto one of the least of these, you have done it unto me."

There's something else we can do with our hands as Christians — we can join our hands. Do you remember as a child how many games began by someone saying, "Now join hands and make a circle"? The world we live in today is torn asunder by hatred and hostility. But in Jesus Christ, we are reminded that we are one family in the sight of God. Do you recall that simple poem about "hands"?

*Christ has no hands but our hands to do his work today,*
*Christ has no feet but our feet to lead others in the way,*

*Christ has no tongue but our tongue to tell others how*
*he died,*
*And Christ has no love but our love to bring others to*
*his side.*

## Closing Prayer

O God, as you once revealed yourself to Thomas by a show of your nail-scarred hands, allow us to share the love of Jesus with others through our consecrated hands.

## Benediction

May God bless you and keep you. May God's face shine on you and be gracious to you. May God look upon you with favor and give you peace. Amen.

# 2. Refreshing Christians

**Greeting and Call To Worship**

*I was glad when they said unto me, "We will go into the house of the Lord."*

**Opening Prayer**

God of wondrous grace, we come thankfully into your presence in these moments of worship. We praise you for the gift of love you have shown us in Jesus Christ. By your Spirit, help us to love one another as you have loved us. Amen.

**Lord's Prayer**

**Special Hymn**                              "Jesus, Lover Of My Soul"

The writer of this hymn was Charles Wesley, who, with his brother John, was a reformer and founder of the Methodist Church. Charles Wesley wrote over 6,500 hymns during his lifetime. He wrote while traveling on horseback; he wrote a hymn on his wedding day; and he even dictated the words of a hymn as he lay dying. Many people think this hymn about Jesus' love was inspired during a terrible storm at sea.

**Scripture Reading**                                    2 Timothy 1:8-18

**Meditation**

Picture in your mind this scene: there is an ancient Roman prison. A soldier in uniform walks up and down in front of a cell. Occasionally, he peers through the doorway at an old man who has been a prisoner there for the past two years. At first this older man was not like the other prisoners. There was a spring in his step and a gleam in his eye as he busied himself writing letters at the rough table in his cell.

But lately, the old man's health has failed. The guard has known from the very beginning that this man must be a person of tremendous faith in God, but today, as the guard looks on, the old man sits dejectedly. He has not touched his food and a look of discouragement is on his face.

Then there is a knock at the gate. The guard quickly recognizes an ordinary-looking man who has come many times to visit the old man in the cell. Inwardly the guard rejoices, for he knows that even a short visit from this friend will cheer the prisoner's heart. The guard watches as the visitor, whose name is Onesiphorus, greets the Apostle Paul with a warm embrace.

The two talk quietly of old times and, before long, they lift up their voices in praise to God. Then they kneel in prayer. There is another embrace and it is time for Onesiphorus to leave. But the guard cannot help noticing the renewed confidence and hopefulness in his prisoner. He watches as the old man rushes to his writing table to scribble something down. Later in the day the guard reads the words the old man was so eager to write: "May the Lord grant mercy to the household of Onesiphorus ... for he often refreshed me."

Now it is those words, "He often refreshed me," that suggest a ministry to which all followers of Jesus Christ are called — the ministry of refreshment. Think for a moment how a cool breeze or a cold drink refreshes us on a hot day. All Christians, regardless of their age, have the opportunity just like Onesiphorus to bring spiritual refreshment to those around them.

Look for a moment at the things Onesiphorus did for Paul. Notice that he came to Paul personally. He didn't just send a card or mutter something about "praying for you." He took the time to come in person. He realized how even the strongest of us can become discouraged and disheartened by life. So he came personally to bring the love of Christ to his friend.

Secondly, Onesiphorus gave Paul a word of appreciation and affirmation. It is amazing how we often wait until someone has died before we say how much that person has meant to us. How much a word of appreciation or affirmation can mean when we face a difficult situation. I recall standing at an airport ticket counter when the customer at the desk gave the airline attendant a beastly time. You could feel the tension in the air as the next customer stepped up to the desk. But to everyone's amazement, the customer looked at the frazzled airline attendant and said, "I certainly admire your patience. You handled that difficult person like a pro!" What a change!

But what really refreshed Paul was that Onesiphorus offered his friend genuine sympathy. Now "sympathy" is not the same as "pity." Sympathy is much more than feeling sorry for someone; it literally means to come alongside another and to suffer his pain with him. Onesiphorus refreshed the great Apostle Paul, and you and I have the same unique opportunity to be refreshing Christians with those around us.

## Closing Prayer

O God, all around us are people who are lonely and discouraged. Give us the eyes to see and the hearts to love others as Christ has loved us. We pray in Jesus' name. Amen.

## Benediction

May the Lord watch between me and thee when we are absent one from another.

# 3. When Life Breaks Your Heart

**Greeting and Call To Worship**
*The heavens are telling the glory of God, and the firmament shows forth God's handiwork to all the nations!*

**Opening Prayer**
God of the universe, we marvel at the beauty of your creation, and the wonder that such a great God has come to us here on earth in the person of Jesus Christ. We praise you that at all times you are our refuge and our strength. In Jesus' name we pray. Amen.

**Lord's Prayer**

**Special Hymn**                                              "Rock Of Ages"
The writer of this favorite hymn, Augustus Toplady, was ordained as a minister in the Church of England when he was just 22 years old. It is said that once when he was traveling through England, he found himself in a terrible storm. Nearby there was a great cleft in the rock, and Augustus Toplady took shelter from the storm in that cleft. As he waited out the storm, the words for this great hymn came to his mind.

**Scripture Reading**                                      2 Corinthians 4:7-9

**Meditation**
The sportscasters on *Monday Night Football* were talking one time about Walter Payton, the great running back of the Chicago Bears. One of them said, "Payton gained more than nine miles rushing the football in his career." There was a brief pause, and then one of the other broadcasters said, "And to think, every 4.6 yards of that nine miles, someone was knocking him down!"

Knockdowns come not only in football but also in life. Life seems to have a way of breaking our hearts. There's the job we

17

wanted but never got. There's the accident that crippled one of our legs, or the heart-wrenching death of a loved one. There's the disappointment some experience as a parent in their children, or the frustration of getting older that most of us experience. Life brings knockdowns — broken dreams and often broken hearts. How do we as Christians respond when life breaks our hearts?

Some people respond to heartache with self-pity. They spend their days feeling sorry for themselves, or just throwing in the towel on whatever has defeated them. There's an old story of passengers on a big 747 airliner halfway across the Atlantic. The pilot tells them that one engine has quit and they will be arriving an hour later than expected in London. In a little while, the pilot tells the passengers he has lost two more engines, but not to worry. They will make it about three hours behind schedule. One self-pitying passenger who had been complaining the whole time said aloud, "Oh, for Pete's sake, if we lose the other engine, we'll be up here all night!"

Self-pity destroys life. It often robs us of our sense of humor; more importantly, it blocks out the voice of God. When life breaks your heart, self-pity is of very little help. Nor is the response of resentment and anger. People who respond to life's heartache with resentment are like Job's wife — they simply advise cursing God and dying. I remember a car dealer I once knew who used to sell those old gas-guzzling luxury cars for a living. But then came the gas shortages, and he lost his dealership. He became a bitter, angry man, and eventually lost his family, his church, his friends, and finally his life.

Paul suggests there is another way to meet those times when life breaks your heart. It is the way of trust. Paul did not blame God for all the misfortunes he experienced. Instead he saw God as a source of strength and help in the midst of his suffering. He somehow grasped the wondrous truth that when we human beings suffer, God suffers with us!

William Barclay, the great Scottish biblical scholar, faced a terrible blow when his beautiful 21-year-old daughter and her fiance were drowned in a boating accident a few weeks before their wedding. Listen to how Barclay's trust in God helped him face that knockdown: "God did not stop that accident at sea ... but God did still the storm in my own aching heart, and gave to me and my wife the strength to come through that terrible time. My comfort is in knowing that the day my daughter was lost at sea, there was sorrow in the heart of God as well as in my own." God does not offer us explanations for life's heartaches, but God does offer us the strength to bring us through the storms of life.

## Closing Prayer

O God, our Rock, give us the grace to trust you even in those moments when we do not understand why the tragedies of life have come to us. May we find you to be, as the Psalmist of old did, our refuge and our strength and a very present help in time of need. Amen.

## Benediction

The Lord bless you and keep you. The Lord make God's face to shine upon you and be gracious to you. The Lord look upon you with favor and give you peace.

# 4. The Shadow You Cast

**Greeting and Call To Worship**
*Make a joyful noise to the Lord, all ye lands; serve the Lord with gladness. Come into God's presence with singing!*

**Opening Prayer**
O God, we thank you for this great and mysterious gift called life. Allow us in these moments of worship together to know you as our Lord and as our Friend. Surround us with your love, that we may be free truly to live. In Jesus' name we pray. Amen.

**Lord's Prayer**

**Special Hymn**                "What A Friend We Have In Jesus"
This wonderful old hymn was written by an Irish composer named Joseph Scriven. Early in his life Scriven discovered how much he needed the friendship of Jesus Christ. The young woman to whom he was engaged tragically drowned on the eve of their wedding. Joseph moved to Canada, where news of his mother's illness back in Ireland reached him. Unable to return, he wrote the words of this hymn as a poem for his mother, hoping it would remind her of Christ's ever-present friendship.

**Scripture Reading**                                    Acts 5:12-16

**Meditation**
Our lives often influence those around us in ways far beyond anything we ever intended. That was certainly true for Peter. As he walked to the great Temple, families with loved ones who were ill would bring their relatives on pallets in the hope that just the shadow of Peter's body would bring healing or some blessing to them. Peter was probably not even aware of their intent; nonetheless, God used Peter's shadow for good.

It is amazing how the unconscious influence of one life upon another has often been the vehicle through which faith in Christ is passed from one generation to the next. Let us trace the course of a remarkable chain of such influences. It was a snowy Sunday morning in Colchester, England, in the year 1850. A boy of fifteen could not get to his own church and had slipped into the balcony of another. A lay person led the service that day because even the preacher was snowed in. His message was the repetition of the text, "Look unto me and be ye saved, all the ends of the earth." It was not much of a sermon, but it touched that boy's heart, so that in time this boy, Charles Haddon Spurgeon, became the greatest preacher in the nineteenth century.

Spurgeon preached in churches and even in open fields, and the impact of his preaching touched many lives. A young man living in America heard of Spurgeon, and managed to work his passage on a ship to Europe so that he could hear Charles Spurgeon. He went everywhere Spurgeon spoke and finally came back to the United States saying, "I went to work to preach like that myself." The young man's name was Dwight L. Moody, whose work as an evangelist literally changed the face of America.

Once when Moody was scheduled to preach in London, a young medical student slipped into the back of the room. On the podium a pastor was giving a long, drowsy prayer. Bored, the young medical student turned to go when suddenly Moody stood up and said, "While our good brother here is finishing his prayer, the rest of us will sing hymn 22!" The young student stayed to hear Moody preach, and his heart was so touched that night, he gave his life to missions. His name was Wilfred Grenfell, and he touched hundreds of lives with his skill as a doctor and his life as a Christian.

Such is the influence we can have for Christ upon one another. It may be something as simple as a smile, a touch, a word, or a look, but it can be a life-changing moment for the person who receives it. It is important to note that in Peter's case, his shadow only became a powerful influence for good when his life was centered in Christ. Nobody was helped by Peter's shadow that night in the courtyard of the High Priest when Peter denied his Lord three times! But when Peter turned his life over to Jesus, even the shadow of his body was a blessing to others. Think about the shadow you cast. Perhaps, like Peter's, God can use it to bless someone around you.

**Closing Prayer**

Gracious God, let our lives be centered in you, so that your Spirit can touch those around us with the love of Jesus Christ. Amen.

**Benediction**

May God bless you and keep you. May God's face shine on you and be gracious to you. May God look upon you with favor and give you peace. Amen.

# 5. Prayer Is For Real!

**Greeting and Call To Worship**
*Jesus said: "Come to me, all you who are heavy laden, and I will give you rest."*

**Opening Prayer**
Lord Jesus, we who are so often heavy laden come into your presence this day. Grant us rest for our weariness, forgiveness for our sin, and strength for all we must face in life. We pray in the name of Jesus, our Lord. Amen.

**Lord's Prayer**

**Special Hymn**                                        "Sweet Hour Of Prayer"
The words to this wonderful old hymn were written by an English lay person who owned a small trinket shop in Coleshill, England. William Walford often served as a lay preacher in many of the churches in that area. One day in 1842, a friend stopped in his shop and Walford asked him to write down a poem he had just completed in his mind, titled "Sweet Hour Of Prayer." The reason Walford asked his friend to write down the words was that he himself was blind. Walford was a person who knew firsthand the power of prayer.

**Scripture Reading**                                        Matthew 6:5-13

**Meditation**
Prayer is probably the most talked about and least practiced subject in the Christian church today. Do you recall the story of the old man out in a rowboat who got caught in a terrible storm? The waves washed away first one oar, and then another. As his little boat filled with water, the man lifted his eyes to heaven and said, "O Lord, I haven't bothered you in the last 25 years. Get me out of this mess, and I won't bother you for 25 more!"

Like that old man in the boat, many of us only pray in dire emergencies. Yet we talk about prayer all the time. There are study groups on prayer, sermons on prayer, prayer meetings, and prayer vigils, but in spite of all our talk, prayer is a very underutilized part of our spiritual lives. One thing is for certain, however. Prayer is for real! Why else did Jesus' disciples want to know more about prayer, except they saw what happened to their Lord every time he prayed?

For many of us, our biggest frustration with prayer is that it seems as if a lot of our prayers go unanswered. In the Lord's Prayer, Jesus reminds us that selfish prayers seldom get answered. There was a little girl who decided to skip her bedtime prayers. When asked why, she said simply, "There are some nights when I do not need a single thing!" God answers our prayers in one of four ways: "Yes," "No," "Wait," or "Have I got a surprise for you!" But we will hear the "No" answer most often until we get ourselves off center stage and realize that prayer is about doing God's will, not our own.

Here is a little verse that speaks to our selfish prayers:

> *You cannot pray the Lord's Prayer and even once say*
> *"I."*
> *You cannot pray the Lord's Prayer and even once say*
> *"My."*
> *Nor can you pray the Lord's Prayer and not pray for*
> *one another,*
> *And when you ask for daily bread, you must include*
> *your brother.*
> *For others are included ... in each and every plea,*
> *From the beginning to the end of it, it does not once*
> *say "Me."*

The real lesson about prayer that Jesus taught his disciples was the importance of trusting God. All of our prayers should contain two important phrases: (1) In Jesus' name — meaning, is what I am asking pleasing to our Lord? and (2) Not my will but thine be done. The Catechism of the United Church of Canada says this about prayer:

24

*Prayer is laying our lives open to God ... casting our-*
*selves on the mercy of God ... telling God the desires of*
*our hearts ... and accepting God's way in our lives.*

Prayer is for real, but the secret of its power lies in the surrender of our wills to the Living God. In the twelve-step program used
by Alcoholics Anonymous, the most fundamental step is this: "We
made a decision to turn our will and our lives over to the care of
God..."

## Closing Prayer

O God, we thank you for the gift of prayer. Forgive us for
focusing so much on our own needs, and not turning our hearts
fully over to you. Teach us the wonder and the power of time spent
in prayer with you each day. May we discover as did the disciples
of old that prayer is for real. Amen.

## Benediction

May the grace of the Lord Jesus Christ, the love of God, and
the communion of the Holy Spirit be with you, both now and forevermore. Amen.

# 6. Amazing Grace

**Greeting and Call To Worship**
*For God so loved the world that God sent the only begotten Son, that all who believe in him should not perish, but have everlasting life!*

**Opening Prayer**
God of love, we praise you for sending your Son into this world to rescue us from our brokenness and our sin. We praise you that your love is so great, you remove our sins from us as far as the east is from the west. O God, grant to our hearts in these moments of worship the gift of your amazing grace. In Jesus' name. Amen.

**Lord's Prayer**

**Special Hymn**                                        "Amazing Grace"
This is a hymn where the hymn writer, John Newton, is writing out of his own experience of God's gracious love. Newton was born in 1725. His mother was a pious woman who taught her son the scriptures. His father was a sea captain and young John longed to join his father at sea. But he soon clashed with his father, found fault with his employers, and ended up in jail. Released, he continued a life of wild and immoral living, and for some years served as the captain of a slave ship. It took a terrifying storm at sea and his deliverance from a malignant fever to make John Newton willing to accept the gift of God's grace.

**Scripture Reading**                                        Joshua 2:1-15

**Meditation**
In God's eyes, what constitutes true greatness? The Bible's answer may surprise you! Take, for example, the story of Rahab, the great, great, great, great, great grandmother of Jesus of Nazareth. Yes, you heard correctly! Rahab was a woman of the night, a madam

who operated an establishment of prostitution in ancient Jericho, and an ancestor of Jesus Christ!

The people of Israel were poised to enter the Promised Land, so Joshua sent some undercover men into the city to gather intelligence, and somehow these spies ended up at Rahab's establishment. When the King of Jericho discovered strangers asking too many questions, he sent his troops to Rahab's to arrest them. But Rahab, knowing these strangers were here on God's business, sent the soldiers away and then helped the spies make their escape. So grateful were the spies that they promised Rahab that nothing would happen to harm her or her family in the coming attack.

Rahab is very typical of the heroes of the Bible, for all of God's heroes seem to have a dark side to their lives. Recall the story of how Abraham lied to the ruler of Egypt about Sarah's being his wife just to save his own skin. Jacob, his nephew, was the modern equivalent of a junk bond salesman! Moses spent a year of his life hiding in the wilderness after committing murder in a fit of anger. Samson for most of his life was a playboy; and David, Israel's greatest King, was willing to commit murder to cover his own adulterous relationship with Bathsheba.

You see, God is not looking for perfect people. God, in fact, seems to choose people with feet of clay, so that when they follow God's purpose, the glory belongs not to them but to the Living God. I recall reading an incident in the life of Abraham Lincoln, one of the greatest of all of our presidents. Yet even Lincoln must have had his moments. It is recorded one night that Mr. Lincoln forcibly ejected Mrs. Lincoln from their home, muttering, "Madam, you make this house intolerable!"

But you see, God never allows that dark side in human nature to diminish our worth in the service of Christ. We make judgments about other people, but with God, you cannot count anyone out! God can use the tightwad, the egotist, the alcoholic, the hypocrite, and in John Newton's case, even a slave trader in his purpose. Newton did not become a minister until he was 39 years old. He spent the rest of his life in Christ's service, and on his tombstone he had these words written:

*John Newton, clerk, once an Infidel and Libertine, a servant of slavers in Africa, was, by the rich Mercy of our Lord and Saviour Jesus Christ, preserved, restored, pardoned, and appointed to preach the faith he had long labored to destroy.*

Whenever you doubt your worth and value as a person, remember that the God who worked through Rahab, the prostitute, and Moses, the murderer, and Paul, the persecutor, can work in your life through the power of amazing grace!

## Closing Prayer

God of grace, we accept the gift of your unmerited favor and love. Fill us with the Spirit of Jesus Christ, that we may serve you and your Kingdom through every day of our lives. In Jesus' name. Amen.

## Benediction

May God bless you and keep you. May God's face shine on you and be gracious to you. May God look upon you with favor and give you peace. Amen.

# 7. What's The Use Of Worrying?

**Greeting and Call To Worship**
*This is the day which the Lord has made; let us rejoice and be glad in it!*

**Opening Prayer**
Lord, like Martha of old in the biblical story, we are anxious and troubled about many things. Help us to take our eyes off our troubles and, instead, to focus on Jesus Christ. May we find courage, strength, wisdom, and mercy as we worship together this day. We pray in Jesus' name. Amen.

**Lord's Prayer**

**Special Hymn**                    "God Will Take Care Of You"
The words of this wonderful old hymn were written by a pastor's wife. Here is the story: Once when the Reverend W. Stillman Martin was invited to preach in New York City, his wife became ill and was unable to accompany him. He was so concerned about her health that he thought of canceling his trip. But the couple's nine-year-old son spoke up and said, "Daddy, don't you think that if God wants you to preach today, he will take care of Mother while you are away?" Martin kept his preaching engagement and when he returned home, his wife had written the beautiful words of "God Will Take Care Of You."

**Scripture Reading**                            Matthew 6:25-34

**Meditation**
Many people will probably recall the song featured for years on the John Gambling radio program, "Pack Up Your Troubles In Your Old Kit Bag, And Smile, Smile, Smile!" Most of us wish it were that easy, but the truth is that almost all of us worry far too

much. We worry about what we have done and what we have failed to do. We worry about what we have said ... and what we should have said. We worry about money, about our children and grandchildren. We worry about our health and about how we will manage as we get older. And as if that were not enough, a lot of us worry about worrying too much!

Jesus knew that worry and anxiety can seriously damage the human spirit and rob us of the joy God intended for us to experience in our lives on this earth. In the Sermon on the Mount, Jesus suggests a simple formula for bringing worry under control.

Our Lord begins by suggesting that we learn to live one day at a time. He tells his disciples, "Tomorrow will be anxious for itself." We need to let go both of our past with all its failures and blunders and our future that has not even arrived. Instead, we are to live, as one writer puts it, "in daytight compartments." There is a story from an old *McGuffey Reader* about a clock on the wall that began thinking of how many times it would have to tick in the year ahead. The clock counted up the seconds — 31,536,000 of them! The thought of what lay ahead was too much for the clock, so it stopped ticking. Then along came someone who reminded the clock that all it had to do was to tick one second at a time. When the clock realized this, it went happily back to ticking, one second at a time. That's the way Jesus means for us to live our lives.

A second part of Jesus' formula for controlling worry is to remember how much God cares for us. He mentions God's care for the lilies of the field and the birds of the air, and then asks how much more God is ready to do for the human family. There was a childhood poem that expressed this truth in a way I have never forgotten:

> *Said the robin to the sparrow, "I should really like to know*
> *Why these anxious human beings rush around and worry so."*
> *Said the sparrow to the robin, "Friend, I think that it must be*
> *They have no Heavenly Father such as cares for you and me."*

Our Lord's final suggestion was to put God first in our living every day. "Seek first the Kingdom of God, and all the rest will be added unto you." Overcoming worry and anxiety according to Jesus is fundamentally a question of where we focus our lives. An old hymn puts this truth so well: "Turn your eyes upon Jesus, look full in his wonderful face; and the things of earth will grow strangely dim, in the light of his glory and grace."

**Closing Prayer**

O God, let us move into each new day in the assurance that you are with us in everything we face. Forgive our failures in the past. Give us the strength we need for today. Allow us to face the future in the confidence that we may not know what is coming, but we do know for sure that Christ will be there to help us face it. In Jesus' name we pray. Amen.

**Benediction**

Go in peace and serve the Lord. May the blessing of God Almighty, Father, Son, and Holy Spirit be with you. Amen.

# 8. The Gospel Of The Second Chance

### Greeting and Call To Worship
*Bless the Lord, O my soul, and all that is within me, bless God's Holy Name!*

### Opening Prayer
God of grace, we come into your presence knowing that all have sinned and come short of the glory of God. Yet, in your mercy, you have promised to forgive us and make us whiter than snow. Let this good news of our faith fill our hearts with praise and thanksgiving as we worship you. We pray in the name of Jesus our Lord. Amen.

### Lord's Prayer

### Special Hymn          "Just As I Am, Without One Plea"
Charlotte Elliott, the author of this hymn, was an invalid much of her life. In the year 1834 Miss Elliott was living in Brighton in her native England. She was 45 years old and had been a devoted Christian for many years. Even so, she was plagued with unhappiness over her seeming uselessness, for everyone around her was busy in the service of God. In her extreme depression, she was tempted to doubt the reality of her spiritual life. Gathering strength and resolve, she decided to make a list of the reasons for trusting in Jesus Christ. The result was the text of this wonderful hymn.

### Scripture Reading          Acts 15:36-41; 2 Timothy 4:11

### Meditation
There is a person in the New Testament whose struggle with faith can be a great source of encouragement to us. His name was John Mark, and most scholars believe he is the author of the Gospel that bears his name. His story is like a drama in four short scenes.

Scene 1 is about his start in the Christian faith. Mark's mother, Mary, was most likely the one who put her home in Jerusalem at Jesus' disposal. It was in the Upper Room of that home where Jesus and his disciples ate the Last Supper together. Mark grew up around those first followers of Jesus. He may even have been a secret disciple who was there with the Twelve on that last night. The Bible tells about a young man who, when Jesus was arrested, slipped out of his clothing and ran away naked into the night! Perhaps that young man was Mark.

Scene 2 describes Mark's faltering in his life as a Christian. Paul and Barnabas have been chosen by the young Christian Church to be the first missionaries, and they decide to take a young and enthusiastic John Mark with them. But in the midst of that first missionary journey, the going gets really rough. The missionaries are not always warmly received. They are traveling in the heat of the summer, and are facing a very rough journey over the mountains when John Mark decides to quit and go home. The Bible says simply, "John left them and returned to Jerusalem." Someone has suggested that at this point, Mark is a disciple with a backbone of spaghetti! He made a good start, but he could not see it through.

Scene 3 describes his bitter disappointment. Years have passed and Mark has matured. He feels he is now ready for missionary work and is eager to prove himself to Paul. But when he signs up for another trip, "Paul thought it best not to take John Mark who had deserted them in Pamphylia." That must have been an awful blow to Mark, but perhaps he learned something about having to live with the consequences of his actions.

Scene 4 describes his restoration as a Christian. Years have passed and Paul has been in Rome in prison. From Rome he writes to Timothy, saying, "Get Mark and bring him with you, for he has been very useful in serving me." That one sentence speaks volumes about the gospel of the second chance. John Mark may have stumbled in his walk of faith, but God's grace is so strong that Mark was restored and forgiven. No wonder this young man was eager to write the story of Jesus and his ministry! He had experienced the love of Jesus firsthand!

The novelist A. J. Cronin was once a doctor in Wales. One night he instructed a young nurse to be sure to clear a breathing tube in her patient before seeking other help. In the night the patient had difficulty breathing. The young nurse panicked. Instead of clearing the tube, she ran for help and the patient died. She pleaded with Cronin for just one more chance. At first, he refused her, but then he remembered how Christ died to give us a second chance, and the next day he forgave that young nurse for her failure. She went on to become the superintendent of the largest children's hospital in Britain. Truly, our faith is based on the gospel of the second chance!

## Closing Prayer

O God, we give thanks that nothing can ever separate us from your love in Christ. We come, just as we are, to experience again your grace and mercy. Renew our faith, cleanse our hearts, and send us forth to serve our Living Lord.

## Benediction

The grace of the Lord Jesus Christ be with you all. Amen.

# 9. Swift To Hear
# And Slow To Speak

**Greeting and Call To Worship**
*The Lord is in God's Holy Temple; let all the earth keep silence before the Lord!*

**Opening Prayer**
Lord, we come into your presence with reverent and believing hearts. Silence the noise and clamor of the world around us, and make our hearts receptive to the voice of your Holy Spirit. Allow us, we pray, to be still and know that you are the Living God. We pray in the name of Jesus our Lord. Amen.

**Lord's Prayer**

**Special Hymn**                                    "I Need Thee Every Hour"
The writer of this hymn was a homemaker going about her daily tasks in April of 1872 when she was filled with a sense of God's presence near to her. Anne Sherwood Hawks was suddenly overwhelmed by the assurance that God was with her both in her times of pain and her times of joy. That day she wrote the poem, "I Need Thee Every Hour," and took it to her pastor, the Reverend Robert Lowry, a noted composer. He recognized the potential of the words and composed the melody we still sing today. Mrs. Hawks wrote many other hymns, but this simple message of relying on God each and every day has proven to be an inspiration to countless Christians over the years.

**Scripture Reading**                              James 1:19-25; 3:1-12

**Meditation**
Perhaps you recall the old story about the pastor who was so concerned one Sunday morning about his sermon that he cut himself while shaving. He put a large Band-aid® on the cut and went to

church. After the service he was standing at the door greeting the parishioners when someone said, "Pastor, what happened to you?" The pastor replied somewhat sheepishly, "I was so concerned about my sermon, I cut myself while shaving this morning." There was a moment of silence and then a voice said, "Next time, do us all a favor, Pastor. Save your face and just cut the sermon!"

It is not only pastors, however, who are accused of talking too much. The writer of the Epistle of James reminds all of us about the importance of speaking and listening. Being able to communicate with other people requires both, and James is very concerned that most of us talk a lot more than we listen. In fact, we are often so intent on what we have to say that we only hear what we want to hear!

Four women were playing bridge in the recreation room of a California retirement center. Suddenly they noticed a rather handsome older gentleman who had just come into the room. One of the women looked up from the bridge table and said, "Hello! You must be new here. I don't recall meeting you." The handsome man responded, "Just moved in this morning." A second lady at the card table asked, "Well, where did you come from?" Without a moment's hesitation, the handsome man replied, "From San Quentin Prison! I have just been released from there after thirty years." "Oh my," said a third lady at the table, "what were you in for?" The older man calmly replied, "I murdered my wife." Whereupon the fourth lady at the bridge table sat up in her chair, and flashing the older man a great big smile, she said, "Oh, that means you must be single!"

Is it not amazing how often we hear only what we want to hear? We are living in a time when we have the technology to listen to a baby while it is still in its mother's womb, or we can listen to the sounds of life on the ocean floor or even on some distant planet. But so very often, we cannot hear the people around us. Even more important, with all our talking and our busyness, we often cannot hear the voice of God.

But the writer of James has yet another caution for us in this matter of speaking and listening. He says to us: "Be sure in your speech that you say what you mean, and mean whatever it is you say." He reminds us that the tongue may be among the smallest parts of the human body, but it is like the tiny spark that ignites a huge forest fire, or the tiny rudder that steers a great ocean liner.

A new pastor was invited to the home of a church officer for dinner. Anxious to make a good impression, the pastor was very complimentary about the dinner that his host served. Then came the dessert. It was a huge piece of rhubarb pie. Now the pastor had learned to eat most everything, but he could not stand rhubarb pie! Believing it was important not to make a fuss, he somehow managed to eat the pie. He seemingly ate it with such joy that he was served another piece! Worst of all, it spread all over the parish that the new pastor's favorite dessert was rhubarb pie! So let us be careful in our daily walk with Christ that we say what we mean and mean what we say.

### Closing Prayer

O God, we need your presence with us through each hour of the day. Help us to learn to be better listeners and to let our lives show forth the same truth that we proclaim with our mouths. In Jesus' name. Amen.

### Benediction

May the blessing of God Almighty, Father, Son, and Holy Spirit, be with you and remain with you both this day and forever. Amen.

# 10. Incredible Faith

**Greeting and Call To Worship**
*I will lift my eyes to the hills. From whence does my help come?*
*My help comes from the Lord, who made heaven and earth!*

**Opening Prayer**
We give thanks, O God, for the gift of faith. We know that it is our faith that sustains us through both joy and sorrow. We confess that at times our faith wavers, but we pray that you would nourish this gift of faith in our hearts. Let it be our faith in Jesus Christ that enables us to live a life of both compassion and justice. We pray in the name of Jesus, our Lord. Amen.

**Lord's Prayer**

**Special Hymn**                    "My Faith Looks Up To Thee"
The writer of this hymn, Ray Palmer, was a direct descendant of John Adams and his wife, Abigail. Poverty forced Palmer to leave home when he was only a boy of thirteen. He became a follower of Jesus Christ while employed as a clerk in a Boston dry goods store. Friends saw his intellectual ability and urged him to attend school. He graduated eventually from Yale University and taught for several years in New York. It was at the age of 22 that Palmer, then living in New York, wrote the words of what many people consider the finest American Christian hymn. It reflects Palmer's own trust in Christ in both the joys and the sorrows of his life.

**Scripture Reading**                    Luke 7:1-10

**Meditation**
There is a wonderful old story about a man climbing a huge mountain, who suddenly loses his footing. He tumbles down into a large canyon, wildly clutching at anything to break his fall. Luckily

he grabs hold of a tiny branch growing out of the rock. Hanging on for dear life, he looks down and realizes he is suspended a good hundred feet above the canyon floor. He looks up at the heavens and shouts, "Is there anybody up there who can help me?" A booming voice from the sky says, "I will help you, my son, but you must have faith. First I want you to let go of the branch you are holding." There is a long silence, and then the mountain climber looks up and says, "Is there anybody **ELSE** up there who can help me?"

Sometimes we all feel like that man hanging on for dear life. If we are honest about it, our faith in Christ is shaken as we read almost every day of terrorist attacks on innocent people, drunk drivers taking the lives of children, and women being assaulted by people they thought they could trust. Genuine faith is not easy to maintain in a world where cruelty, injustice, and greed seem to be in control. That's one reason why our ears perk up when we hear Jesus saying to this Roman soldier, "I have never seen a stronger faith in all of Israel." What was it about this Roman's faith that made it so incredible?

Let's begin with the fact that it was his faith that made this centurion so kind and compassionate. If you study the Gospels carefully, you will discover that Jesus' test of real faith is how much compassion and kindness it produces in a human life. According to Jesus, that is how you measure faith. This solder's compassion for his sick slave was amazing in the ancient world. Slaves were not even considered to be persons. They were mere tools to be used and then discarded. With no thought for himself or his reputation, this proud Roman reaches out to Jesus for help.

In our often cold and self-centered world, we find this ancient centurion's faith a real source of inspiration. There is a famous *Peanuts* cartoon which shows Linus watching his favorite television program when his sister Lucy enters the room and abruptly changes the channel! Linus says, "Hey, Lucy, I was here first!" Lucy responds, "Linus, it says in the twentieth chapter of Matthew's Gospel that the first shall be last, and the last shall be first." Linus ponders this for a moment and then says, "I'll bet anything Matthew didn't have an older sister!"

But there is a second quality to this Roman's faith that is equally important — his faith made him not only compassionate but just. Jews and Gentiles in the first century were sworn enemies. They had almost nothing to do with each other. Yet this Roman centurion obviously had cultivated a fair and just relationship with the people. We learn that he had even helped the Jewish people build a synagogue in Capernaum. Faith in Jesus Christ requires of us not only that we do acts of kindness, but that we fight against the greed and the injustice that seem to dominate the headlines each day.

There is an old saying that "going to church on Sunday is no good unless your faith makes you honest on Monday." We honor this ancient Roman centurion with his incredible faith that made him both compassionate and just.

## Closing Prayer and Benediction

O God, increase our faith. Like the soldier of old, may it be our faith in Christ Jesus that makes us both compassionate and just in all our relationships. To your name be glory forever and ever. Amen.

# 11. The Ministry Of Encouragement

**Greeting and Call To Worship**
*O sing unto the Lord a new song! Sing unto the Lord, all the earth!*

**Opening Prayer**
Lord, we come into your life-giving presence to be refreshed and empowered by your Holy Spirit. The fears, the worries, and the burdens we carry often discourage our hearts and rob us of the joy you intended for your human family on earth. Drive the dark of our fears away, and fill us with your light, that we may truly sing your praises each day of our lives. In Jesus' name. Amen.

**Lord's Prayer**

**Special Hymn**                    "In My Heart There Rings A Melody"
Elton Menno Roth, the writer of this hymn, was for many years a distinguished church musician. He was known as a singer, composer, and conductor, and he organized choirs of singers which achieved national recognition in their concert tours during the 1930s. This hymn was written while Roth was conducting an evangelistic campaign. On a very hot summer afternoon, Roth took a short walk. Becoming weary with the oppressive heat, he stepped inside the open door of a church. There were no people in the pews and no minister in the pulpit, but as Roth walked up and down the aisle, he began humming this tune and thinking of the words. That same night over 200 boys and girls sang this hymn at an open air meeting. Someone has said, "If there were more singing Christians, there would be a lot more Christians in the world!"

**Scripture Reading**                                    Acts 4:32-37

## Meditation

At some time or other, everyone needs a word of encouragement. All of us are blessed by someone who puts a song back into our hearts or puts the spring back into our step. In the Bible there is a man who was so good at this that his friends began to call him "Son Of Encouragement." Barnabas is not mentioned many times in the Bible, but every time we read his name, he demonstrates for us the ministry of encouragement.

The Bible says of Barnabas, "He was a good man, full of the Holy Spirit and of truth." Now sometimes we call a person "a good man" when we don't know what else to say. There was a preacher who was called upon to bury a very prominent citizen who had seldom attended church. He began his meditation by saying, "Now, Joe was not what you would call a good man, because he never gave his heart to the Lord. But he was you might call a most respected sinner!" In the case of Barnabas, however, he was called "good" because he brought such encouragement to those around him.

Barnabas encouraged others by being a generous giver. He literally saved the early Christian fellowship by selling a piece of land owned and bringing all the proceeds to the Apostles. Barnabas was one of those people who, when he gave his heart to Jesus, also gave his time, his gifts, and his money to the Lord. He was very different from the little girl who met her pastor as she was coming out of the ice cream store on a Sunday morning. The pastor said sternly, "Carol, did you use your offering money for an ice cream cone?" Carol thought for a moment and said, "I figured out that if I buy these super cones, I can let the ice cream man give the money to God!" Not so with Barnabas. His generosity began with himself, and it brought encouragement to those around him.

On another occasion, we find Barnabas encouraging others by his willingness to believe in people when they had a hard time believing in themselves. Barnabas was the first person to believe in Paul after his dramatic conversion experience. Later, when Paul had lost confidence in Mark, it was Barnabas who took young John Mark under his wing as they went off together to the mission field. How wonderful it is when a Christian encourages those around them simply by believing in them. In a world where so many negative things are said, how wonderful it is to have a friend who is positive and encouraging! There was an old woman who was known for never saying a bad word about anyone. One day, a friend said to her, "Mary, I believe you would even say a good word for the devil!" The old woman replied, "Well, you do have to admire his persistence!"

Barnabas was called good for still another reason — he used every opportunity God gave him to share his new faith with others. He became one of the church's first missionaries, and his enthusiasm for Jesus Christ encouraged many people to become Christians. Why is it that when someone is enthusiastic about baseball, we call him a "fan" and that is okay? Yet, when someone gets enthusiastic about his religion, we brand him a "fanatic" and that is all wrong! Barnabas used his whole life to encourage others. "He was a good man, full of the Holy Spirit and of truth."

## Closing Prayer and Benediction

Gracious God, we thank you for those who have brought encouragement into our lives. Fill us with your spirit, that, like Barnabas of old, we may share this ministry of encouragement to all those around us. To you, O God, be all glory and praise. Amen.

# 12. Down In The Dumps

**Greeting and Call To Worship**
*They who wait for the Lord shall renew their strength, they shall mount up with wings like eagles, they shall run and not be weary, they shall walk and not faint!*

**Opening Prayer**
O God, you have promised to be our refuge and our strength. We come to you weighed down by the cares and the burdens of our daily lives. We confess that at times the lamp of faith burns dimly and we are filled with doubt and despair. O God, in your mercy, lift us above our darkness and distress. Renew our faith, and fill us with your Holy Spirit. We pray in Jesus' name. Amen.

**Lord's Prayer**

**Special Hymn**                           "Nearer My God To Thee"
The writer of this old and familiar hymn, Sarah Flower, was born in Harlow, England. She aspired to a career on the stage, but was forced to abandon her plans because of poor health. She married a civil engineer and lived the remaining years of her life in London. Sarah had a sister, Eliza, whom she deeply loved. When Eliza discovered she had tuberculosis, Sarah undertook the care of her sister. It was while caring for Eliza that Sarah discovered her literary gifts. One day she read the story of Jacob's encounter with God in Genesis 28 to her sister. When she finished, the words of this wonderful hymn came to her mind. Through many years, this hymn has brought hope and renewed confidence to God's people.

**Scripture Reading**                           1 Kings 19:1-8

**Meditation**
Would it not be a wonderful thing if life brought us only joy and happiness? Would it not be great to have the attitude of the

young boy whose Little League baseball team was playing a big game? The boy's parents arrived late for the start of the game, and their first question was, "What's the score?" "Oh," said the little boy, "it's 18 to 0, but our team hasn't even come to bat yet!" What a positive outlook that little fellow had!

But life is not that way for most of us. Along with joy come frustration, disappointment, the loss of loved ones, and lots of crises to face. Most of us can identify with the young mother who had one of those awful days that would get anybody down in the dumps. When her husband finally came home, she described all the day's disasters, and said, "And when I finally called Dial-A-Prayer, I got a busy signal!"

Whenever we find ourselves in a low mood, we need to turn to this story of Elijah in the Bible. Elijah was a strong person. He had shown great courage in standing up to the false prophets of King Ahab and Queen Jezebel. But like a lot of us, Elijah was weary from dealing with so many troubles. He was down in the dumps, and in that low mood he asked God to end his life. But God did three things to help his prophet get back on his feet, three things God can still do to help us when we are down in the dumps.

First, God ministered to Elijah's physical needs. He knew that when we get physically exhausted our spirits sink into doubt and depression. So God provided Elijah with food and rest, and it made an immediate difference in Elijah's life. Sometimes we forget in our busy lives that the laws of physical health are also part of God's world. Sometimes a good meal and a good night's rest can change our situation dramatically.

Then God acted to give Elijah a new perspective on his life. The prophet was feeling very sorry for himself. He even tells God that he is the only one in all Israel to remain faithful to the Lord. But God gently turns Elijah's outlook away from himself and his troubles to the fact that God has more than 7,000 persons in Israel who have remained faithful to the Lord! Suddenly, Elijah sees things in a different perspective. Our perspective on life is very important. Do you recall the story of Susan who wrote to her parents from college? She said, "I have decided to leave school and marry Joe. He's just out of jail but he's very good looking. We've known each other for three months, and I know he will be a good father to the baby which arrives in April. Love, Susan. P.S. Dear Folks, I am not leaving school, nor am I pregnant, nor am I dating an ex-con named Joe. But I wrote this letter hoping it would give you a better perspective on the fact that I got an 'F' on my last chemistry test!"

There is one more thing God did to put his prophet back on his feet — God gave Elijah a renewed purpose. He told him he had a job for him to do on God's behalf, and a mission to accomplish. Sometimes we let ourselves get overwhelmed by the evil in this world. But when we undertake some task, no matter how small, in the service of Jesus Christ, our lives take on a whole new meaning and purpose. As the old Chinese proverb reminds us, "It is better to light one candle than to curse the darkness." That is how God ministered to Elijah long ago, and how God can help us when we are down in the dumps.

**Closing Prayer and Benediction**
O God, lift us on eagle's wings that we may renew our strength, and go forth from here in the power of the Holy Spirit. Amen.

# 13. Really Serious Business

**Greeting and Call To Worship**
*But you are a chosen race, a royal priesthood, a holy nation, God's own people, that you may declare the wonderful deeds of him who called you out of darkness into his marvelous light!*

**Opening Prayer**
God of mercy, we thank you for calling us out of the darkness of our sinful lives into the marvelous light of Christ's love and forgiveness. As followers of Jesus, you call us now to be a light to our broken and sinful world. Grant us the grace to live each day for the Living Christ, for we pray in his name. Amen.

**Lord's Prayer**

**Special Hymn**                                        "Trust And Obey"
The music for this hymn was composed by D. B. Towner, the first Director of Music at Moody Bible Institute in Chicago. The inspiration for the hymn's writing came in 1886 at a time when Towner was leading singing for D. L. Moody in Brockton, Massachusetts. During a testimony service Towner heard a young man say, "I am not quite sure — but I am going to trust and I am going to obey." Towner jotted down the words and sent them to a Presbyterian minister friend, J. H. Sammis, who developed the idea into the hymn we now sing. This hymn emphasizes the importance of both faith and good works in living as a Christian.

**Scripture Reading**                                    Mark 9:42-47

**Meditation**
Of all the criticisms made about the Christian Church in America today, none is quite so damning as the often expressed opinion, "The church simply does not matter!" And if the church does not matter to most people in our country, then the fault lies

with those of us who call ourselves Christians, but who fail to take our faith seriously enough to make a difference in the way we live.

Jesus warned his followers on many occasions that being his disciple was a serious matter. Jesus was serious about our sinfulness. He once said, "If your right hand causes you to sin, cut it off." But in our time, people rarely even talk about sin anymore. Dr. Karl Menninger, world-renowned psychiatrist, has written a bestselling book called *Whatever Became Of Sin?* He argues that the moral sickness in America today is the direct result of our failure to take our disobedience to God seriously. Someone has said, "Sin will take you further than you want to go; sin will keep you longer than you want to stay; and sin will cost you more than you want to pay." Jesus took our sinfulness seriously, and so must we.

Jesus was also serious about our beliefs being backed up by our behavior. He knew that it is much easier to talk about being a Christian than it is to live the Christian life on a daily basis. Too many people treat their faith like an old pastor who decided he wanted to become a golfer. He went out one morning with a friend to play golf. On the first tee, he swung the club and missed the ball three times. On his fourth swing, he missed the ball and bent the golf club. On his fifth swing, he hit the ball, but it struck a nearby tree, and bounced back to hit him on the head. The irate minister shouted, "That's it! I quit!" His friend, who had been standing there the whole time, said, "You're giving up golf?" "No," shouted the angry cleric, "I'm quitting the ministry!" Jesus is looking for disciples who will not quit, and who are serious about backing up their beliefs with Christian behavior.

Jesus Christ also told his disciples that he was serious about doing God's will, not his own. In the Lord's Prayer, we pray, "Thy will be done on earth as it is in heaven." But so often our own stubborn wills want things our way instead of God's way. Do you recall the lines of the following poem:

> *I'll go where you want me to go, dear Lord,*
> *I'll say what you want me to say;*
> *I'm busy just now with myself, dear Lord,*
> *I'll try to help you some other day.*

Jesus considers our daily walk of trust and obedience to the Living Christ to be very serious business. With the help of God's Spirit, let's get serious about living our faith in a way that makes a difference.

## Closing Prayer

O God, give us the strength and determination to turn our words into deeds of love and justice. May the world know that we are Christians by our love. We pray in the name of our Lord and Savior, Jesus Christ. Amen.

## Benediction

May God bless you and keep you. May God's face shine on you and be gracious to you. May God look upon you with favor and give you peace.

# 14. On Being In Second Place

**Greeting and Call To Worship**

*If anyone is in Christ, he has become a new creation. The old has passed away; behold, the new has come! To God be the glory and praise!*

**Opening Prayer**

O God, we praise you for coming to us in your Son, Jesus the Christ. Sometimes we feel as if our lives are so unimportant. As we grow older, and are less able to do the things we have usually done, we question our worth and value. Help us to remember that our real worth is based not on what we think or others think of us, but on the fact that the Son of God gave his life for each one of us. We pray in Jesus' name. Amen.

**Lord's Prayer**

**Special Hymn**                                    "To God Be The Glory"

Originally composed in America sometime before 1875, this hymn failed to become popular in this country. It was sung, however, in Great Britain. When Billy Graham held one of his crusades in London in 1954, someone there suggested it be sung. It was so popular with the audience and with Billy Graham's team that it was sung every night during that evangelistic crusade. Returning to America, Billy Graham used this hymn in a meeting in Tennessee in August of 1954. It was as if America rediscovered this great old hymn! Ever since 1954, the people of God have been singing this song which reminds us all that the real praise and glory in the Christian faith belongs to God and not to us!

**Scripture Reading**                                    Acts 1:15-17, 21-26

**Meditation**

There is an old story about a young preacher who was invited to speak one Sunday evening in a neighboring church. He felt very flattered by the invitation until he was being introduced to the congregation. The person in charge told the group that the speaker they really wanted for that night could not come, so this young preacher was their second choice. Pointing to a broken window in the church that had been crudely covered with a piece of cardboard, the man introduced the young preacher by saying, "Our guest tonight is like that cardboard — he's a substitute for the real thing!" The young pastor was somewhat shaken by all this, but he got up and did his best. At the end of the service, an elderly woman said to him, "Son, you weren't a cardboard substitute tonight — you were a real pane!"

We laugh at the predicament of that young preacher, but in almost all of life, most of us have ended up being somebody's second, third, or even fourth choice. Most of us never got to play baseball in the Major Leagues. Most of us never were the president of the company, or the smartest person in our class in school. The vast majority of us are people who never make first place in the eyes of the world.

In the Bible there is a man named Justus who must have known what it feels like to be passed over for promotion, or to end up in second place. After the death of Judas, the Apostles needed to find a replacement. Two men of faith were suggested, Matthias and Justus. The Apostles voted, and Matthias was elected. But how do you think Justus felt? He apparently was qualified, experienced, and deserving, yet someone else was chosen for the top spot. So how do those of us who place second, third, and fourth in life maintain a sense of our value and worth?

My guess is that Justus remembered two very important things about his relationship to Christ. The first is the fact that everyone who has received God's grace in Jesus Christ is worthwhile. Our worth in life is not measured by popular opinion, or Gallup polls, or even our credit rating! Our worth lies in the fact that God counts us valuable enough to let his beloved Son die in our place at Calvary. You and I, no matter what others may think of us, are worth the life of God's own Son! Years ago in Paris, a derelict man was picked up by the police and brought to a hospital half dead. The doctors looked at the man on the table and one of them said in

Latin, "What shall we do with this worthless wretch?" Suddenly, the man on the table opened his eyes, and in flawless Latin said, "Sir, call no one worthless for whom Jesus Christ died!"

The other great thing Justus remembered in his disappointment was that all of us take on a new worth just by being related to Jesus Christ. Think back to when Jimmy Carter was our President. Do you remember hearing about the President's brother Billy? No one would ever have paid a moment's attention to Billy Carter except for one thing — he was the brother of the President of the United States! Our lives take on a whole new value because we are now related by God's grace to the Son of God! So when you get discouraged and feel as if your life is no longer worthwhile, do what Martin Luther used to do. Say to yourself, "I am the friend of Jesus Christ!"

### Closing Prayer and Benediction

God of grace and glory, remind us that it is not who we are or what we have accomplished that is important. What really counts is what you have done for us in Jesus Christ. To your name be all glory and praise, both now and evermore. Amen.

# 15. Christy And Criticism

**Greeting and Call To Worship**
*Let all bitterness and wrath and anger and evil-speaking be put away from you with all malice, and be kind to one another, tenderhearted, forgiving one another, even as God, for Christ's sake, has forgiven you.*

**Opening Prayer**
God of love, we thank you for loving us in spite of our brokenness and sin. We confess that all of us have sinned and fallen short of your glory. Yet, in Jesus Christ, you reach out to us in forgiveness and mercy. O God, let the vision of the life that we see in Jesus become our vision. By the power of your Spirit, let us learn to love one another, even as you love us. We pray in the name of Christ Jesus, our Lord. Amen.

**Lord's Prayer**

**Special Hymn**                                        "Be Thou My Vision"
The hymn "Be Thou My Vision" is really a prayer that we may accept Jesus Christ as the pattern for our lives on earth. The original version of this hymn was written by an unknown Irish Christian in the eighth century. The tune is an Irish folk melody that over the past several decades has become known and loved by Christian people. Perhaps the writer of this hymn was inspired by that often quoted proverb from the wise sayings of King Solomon: "Where there is no vision, the people perish" (Proverbs 29:18). When we sing this hymn, we are asking Jesus to be the "Lord of my heart," "my best thought," and "my true Word."

**Scripture Reading**                                        Luke 6:39-49

**Meditation**
There is an old story about a pastor who preached one day on the Parable of the Talents. This pastor urged all the members of the

53

church to think of at least one talent or gift that they could use in God's service. At the end of the service, a man came up to the pastor and said, "I can't sing in the choir or teach a class, but I do have one talent that I think might be useful in this church. I have the gift of criticism, and I would be happy to criticize the choir, and the church school, and even your sermons! What should I do with my gift?" The pastor was silent for a time and then said, "Friend, do you remember in Jesus' story what the person with only one talent did? He buried his talent in the ground, and frankly, I think you should do the same thing!"

Jesus said, "Judge not that you be not judged," but most of us are often guilty of passing judgments about the people around us. We may not be guilty of the gross sins that land people in jail, but almost all of us have hurt others by being critical and judgmental. The problem with criticism and faultfinding is that it does more to poison the stream of the world's life than most of the crimes we hear about on the evening news. Jesus is not saying that it is wrong to form opinions or make judgments about the issues we all face in life. But he is warning us about one of the worst sins — the critical and careless remarks that often destroy the spirit of those around us. Why is criticism of others so harmful?

One reason to be very careful about criticizing someone else is that time has a way of making fools out of people who open their mouths too quickly to censure others. There was an editor who listened to Lincoln's Gettysburg Address and wrote the next day in his paper: "We pass over the silly remarks of the President. For the credit of the nation, we hope the veil of oblivion will be dropped over them quickly, and they shall no longer be repeated or thought of again." No one even remembers the name of that editor, but who of us can't recall at least the opening words of Lincoln's great speech?

Still another problem with criticism is the way our judgmental remarks about others have a way of coming back to haunt us. I think of that time when two men were at a meeting listening to a woman on the platform singing. One man turned to the other and said, "What a terrible voice that woman has! Do you know who

54

she is?" The other man turned and said quietly, "The woman singing is my wife!" The first man stammered, "Oh, I beg your pardon. It's not really her voice that bothers me — it's that awful music she is singing. I wonder who wrote it?" And the other man replied, "Why, I wrote that music for my wife!"

But perhaps the most important reason for Christians to be careful about criticizing others is God's incredible mercy to all of us. The real motive for being kind to others is not the mercy we hope to receive from God, but the mercy God has already shown us in his Son, Jesus Christ. May the remembrance of how much we need God's love in our own lives make us slow to criticize others, and quick to sympathize with those around us.

### Closing Prayer

O God, forgive us for criticizing others when there is so much in our own lives that needs correcting. Give us the hearts to love others, even as you have loved us in Christ. Amen.

### Benediction

The grace of the Lord Jesus Christ be with you all. Amen.

# 16. Facing A Giant

**Greeting and Call To Worship**

*God is our refuge and strength, and a very present help in time of trouble! Therefore, we will not be afraid!*

**Opening Prayer**

O God, our help in ages past and our hope for years to come, we give thanks for your Living Presence with us in all that we face each day. Sometimes our fears overwhelm us, and our burdens seem greater than we can bear. God of grace, remind us this day that we can do all things through Jesus Christ who strengthens us. We ask this in Jesus' name. Amen.

**Lord's Prayer**

**Special Hymn** "How Firm A Foundation"

When he left the presidency, Andrew Jackson retired to his famous home, the Hermitage, where his many friends often came to visit. On one such occasion, General Jackson said to a local clergyman, "There is a beautiful hymn on the subject of the exceeding great and precious promises of God to us. It was a favorite hymn of my dear wife till the day of her death. It commences: 'How firm a foundation, ye saints of the Lord.' I wish you would sing it now." And so, to please the ex-president, his guests joined in singing this hymn. Although this hymn has been a favorite in America since it appeared in 1787, its authorship is unknown. However, its strong message has brought courage to the hearts of all who sing it.

**Scripture Reading** 1 Samuel 17:37-50

**Meditation**

Everyone knows and loves this old story of David, the young shepherd boy, and his encounter with the Philistine giant, Goliath. But is this just a colorful story from Hebrew history, or can we learn something about facing the giants in our own lives — those obstacles that seem larger than life itself? Our giants, our Goliaths, are not those we meet on a battlefield, but in our doctor's office, or with a phone call in the middle of the night. Our giants take the form of cancer, heart failure, divorce, grief, crushing disappointment, fear, and loss. What can we learn from this old story about facing our giants?

Certainly one obvious truth is the need to face our fears head-on. A lot of us are really good in the crisis moments about saying, "Lord, I want you to use me — especially in an advisory capacity!" But we learn from David that facing up to our giants is the first step in disarming their power over us.

A second truth we can take from this old story is the incredible energy that flows into our lives when we take a stand for that which is good and right. David found great courage in facing his giant, because he believed what he was doing was for the glory of God. Kipling once wrote, "There is only one thing more terrible in battle than a regiment of desperadoes, and that is a company of Scotch Presbyterians who rise from their knees and go into action, convinced that they are about to do the will of God!"

A third truth we can take from this story is the necessity of being yourself as you face your giant. King Saul wanted young David to wear his heavy armor in facing Goliath, but David knew that trying to look like a soldier was not being true to who he really was — a shepherd boy armed with a sling and the power of God. I saw a bumper sticker that said, "God made you, and God knew what He was doing." That is another way of saying, "Be yourself when you go forth to battle a giant."

But the most important truth in this old story is David's trust in God. Listen again to what young David says to mighty Goliath: "You come to me with sword and spear, but I come to you in the name of the Lord!" That was the secret of David's courage and strength — the trust in God's power that had sustained him through all of his life. Most of you will remember the radio show that featured George Burns and his wife, Gracie Allen. In real life, Gracie Allen was a bright, wise businesswoman who shared a wonderful life with her husband George. But often in their comic routines she played the part of a ditsy personality whose sweetly simple approach to life provided many laughs.

In one episode Gracie became very upset because her electric clock kept losing time. So Gracie called a repairman who almost immediately discovered the problem — Gracie's electric clock was not plugged into the outlet! When he told Gracie the problem, she said, "Oh, I know that! I didn't want to waste electricity, so I only plug it in when I want to know what time it is!" A lot of people forget that the resources of God are only there when we are plugged in each day to the Living God. David's whole life was one of faithfulness and trust in the Lord. That's the firm foundation we all need as we face our giants.

### Closing Prayer

O God of power and might, we turn to you as we face the giants in all of our lives. May we, like David of old, find the strength, the courage, and the wisdom we need to be victorious. We pray in the name of Jesus our Lord. Amen.

### Benediction

To you, O God, be all glory and praise, both now and forevermore. Amen.

# 17. When You Feel Inadequate

**Greeting and Call To Worship**

*The hour is coming, and now is, when the true worshipers will worship God in spirit and in truth. God is spirit, and those who worship God must worship in spirit and in truth.*

**Opening Prayer**

Almighty God, we come into your presence with all our needs. We need your mercy to forgive us for our sins. We need strength to bear us up in our weakness. We need your wisdom to guide us in our perplexity. We need your courage to deal with our fears. We need your healing love to mend our broken hearts. O God, touch us with your life-giving Spirit, that we may be renewed in both body and mind in this time of worship. We pray in Jesus' name. Amen.

**Lord's Prayer**

**Special Hymn**                              "How Great Thou Art"

This wonderful hymn comes to us after almost seventy years of literary activity, involving several different writers and translators. The original writer was a Swedish pastor named Carl Gustav Boberg, who was a well-known preacher and religious editor and at one time a member of the Swedish Parliament. His initial title was "O Great God." A resident of Estonia translated the Swedish hymn into German, and from there it traveled to Russia where it was published in a book of Russian evangelical hymns. An English missionary couple, Mr. and Mrs. Stuart Hine, used this hymn in their work in the Ukraine, and then brought an English version back home to England during the Second World War. There they added the final verse, and named the hymn "How Great Thou Art."

**Scripture Reading**                              John 6:1-13

## Meditation

Almost everyone has heard of Michael Jordan, the great basketball player for the Chicago Bulls. Several years ago, in a pressure-packed playoff game, Jordan scored a record high 63 points! A few days after that game another Chicago Bulls player was being interviewed by the press. He was asked what was the highlight of his professional basketball career, and without a moment's hesitation he responded, "I'll never forget the night Michael Jordan and I combined for 65 points!"

Whenever I read this incredible story of Jesus feeding 5,000 hungry people with a little boy's barley loaves and fish, I recall the legend connected with this passage that says the little boy ran all the way home that night and burst into his house saying, "Mama, you'll never guess what Jesus and I did today!"

Do you see the common thread in both of those stories? Wonderful things happen when our little lives are linked with a source of power and greatness. The spiritual lesson in this story is that God can take our little and make it into a lot! If we offer God whatever we have, however inadequate it may seem, God can use it for amazing good.

The real hero in this biblical story is that little boy. If you were to visit the Holy Land today, you would see a wall with a mosaic on it depicting Jesus feeding the 5,000 people. What do you think that the early artist felt was most significant in this story? Was it the abundance of food? Was it the frantic disciples, wringing their hands in the face of so much need? Was it the hungry crowd crying out for bread? No, the central figure in the mosaic is the little boy handing over all he had, his five loaves and two fish, to Jesus. The message is still clear: if we bring whatever we have to the Living Christ, God can still make a lot out of our little!

History is full of examples of faithful women and men who brought to the Lord whatever they had, and dared to trust in our great God for all they needed. An old lady came to Booker T. Washington when he was trying to raise funds for the building of Tuskegee Institute. She was clad in rags, and obviously was a person with a very small income, but this is what she said: "Mr. Washington, God knows I have spent the best years of my life in slavery, and God knows I am ignorant and poor. But I know you are trying to make better men and women for the colored race, so I want you to take these six eggs I have been saving up, and use them to help those children get an education."

Booker T. Washington said afterwards that no other gift he ever received touched him so deeply. The story of that woman's willingness to share what little she had for the advancement of God's Kingdom touched hundreds of other hearts, and their financial gifts made Tuskegee Institute a reality.

So, bring your feelings of inadequacy; bring your worries and your troubles; bring God your time and your abilities no matter how limited they may be; and, most of all, bring God your trusting heart. Then watch as God once more makes a lot out of our little!

## Closing Prayer

Teach us, O Lord, that you are a great God who is more than adequate to meet all of our needs. May we learn to trust you even as a little boy once trusted Jesus enough to give him his lunch in order to feed 5,000 people.

## Benediction

Go now in peace, and know that God goes beside you, showing you the way. Amen.

# 18. Spiritual Cataracts

**Greeting and Call To Worship**
*Jesus said: I am the good shepherd. I know my own and my own know me. He will feed his flock like a shepherd; he will gather the lambs in his arms, and carry them in his bosom.*

**Opening Prayer**
Eternal God, you have led us like a good shepherd through our days and years. Continue to open our eyes to your presence in our lives so that we may not find life empty or lacking in purpose. Fill us with your life-giving Spirit, that we may continue to serve you and glorify your name. Through Jesus Christ our Lord. Amen.

**Lord's Prayer**

**Special Hymn**                    "Open My Eyes That I May See"
The author and composer of this hymn, Clara Scott, lived from 1841 until her death in 1897. For much of her life, she taught music in the Ladies' Seminary in Lyons, Iowa. She wrote many pieces of music both for voice and for instruments, including "The Royal Anthem Book," which was the first collection of Christian anthems published by a woman in this country. This particular hymn was inspired by the words of the Psalmist in the 119th Psalm, verse 18, which uses the phrase, "Open my eyes."

**Scripture Reading**                    Matthew 6:19-24

**Meditation**
One of the annoying problems that many of us face as we get older is the problem of cataracts that form on our eyes. A pamphlet from a doctor's office says this about cataracts: "A cataract is a clouding over of the lens of the eye. This filminess causes a loss of transparency, and obstructs the passage of light into the eye. The result is distorted vision. If left unattended, the cloudiness may

become so heavy that no light can get through the eye, and vision is lost altogether."

Those words about cataracts are very much like the words Jesus once spoke about the "eye." He said, "The eye is the lamp of the body. If your eye is sound, your whole body will be full of light ... but if your eye is not sound, your whole body will be full of darkness." Jesus is talking here not only about our physical ability to see, but also about our whole perspective and outlook on life. It makes a great difference whether we see the glass of water on the table as half full or half empty. The poet put it this way: "Two men looked out through prison bars. One saw mud and the other saw stars!"

As we grow older, there is the danger not only of physical cataracts that distort our vision, but also of spiritual cataracts that cloud our judgment and warp our perspective on all of life. One of those spiritual cataracts we need to be wary about is prejudice. Prejudice can be a terrible thing in the human heart! Just to lump people into groups is blind, unfair, and often very cruel. To think, for example, that all musicians are alike, or all women are alike, or all Southerners are alike is just plain wrong. To think that all teachers, or all African-Americans, or all people with red hair are exactly alike is foolishness. At best, lumping people into narrow categories like that is stereotyping, and, at worst, it can be heartbreakingly cruel. Prejudice in any form is a fundamental denial of the Bible's message that God loves each and every one of us in exactly the same way.

A second spiritual cataract that afflicts many people is closed-mindedness. One of the consequences of a physical cataract is the loss of peripheral vision. A person begins to see in only one direction. The same thing can happen spiritually when people close their minds to new thoughts, new ways of doing things, or new possibilities in their lives. It is like the old saying, "Don't confuse me with the facts ... my mind is already made up!" Someone has pointed out that closed-mindedness is one of the most common sins of church people. He says that the Seven Last Words of the Church are: "We Never Did It That Way Before."

Yet another spiritual cataract we need to avoid is jealousy and resentment. When we carry a grudge or a resentment in our hearts against someone, it can cloud our judgment, distort our vision, and eventually cause us to become spiritually blind. Do you recall Shakespeare's famous play, *Othello*? Othello loved the beautiful Desdemona and she loved him, but Iago planted the seed of jealousy in Othello's mind. That jealousy eventually drove Othello to a blind rage in which he smothered Desdemona to death.

Perhaps you can think of other spiritual cataracts that can destroy our spiritual lives: disappointment, fear, hatred, and selfishness could all be added to the list of enemies of the human spirit. But let us rejoice that in Jesus Christ, God is ready and willing to remove our spiritual cataracts, so that the light of God's love can get through to our hearts.

**Closing Prayer**

> *Open my eyes, that I may see*
> *Glimpses of truth Thou hast for me;*
> *Place in my hands the wonderful key*
> *That shall unclasp and set me free.*
> *Silently now I wait for Thee,*
> *Ready, my God, Thy will to see.*
> *Open my eyes, illumine me, Spirit Divine!*

# 19. When You Need A Life-changing Moment

**Greeting and Call To Worship**
*If anyone is in Christ, he is a new creation. The old has passed away and the new has come. Praise the name of the Lord!*

**Opening Prayer**
God of grace, you continue to bring new life and new possibilities to your people. Forgive us for ever thinking we are too old to change. Remind us that in the power of your Spirit, all things are possible. We pray in the name of Jesus, the Christ. Amen.

**Lord's Prayer**

**Special Hymn**                                  "I Love To Tell The Story"
This hymn was written in 1868 by Katherine Hankey. She was a woman of culture and deep faith in Christ. At an early age, she became interested in Sunday School work in London. Her influence with shop-girls in London was great, and many who attended her Bible classes became members of the church. Some of her best hymns were inspired by her experiences as a Sunday School teacher. In the midst of her work in London, Katherine was called to Africa to nurse an invalid brother. While there she became very interested in mission work, and upon her return to England, she was moved to donate the proceeds of her writings to foreign missions. It was evangelist Dwight L. Moody who popularized this hymn in America.

**Scripture Reading**                                          Luke 19:1-10

**Meditation**
Let me tell you about a man named John who is very bright and successful. He moved up the corporate ladder so quickly, even

he was amazed. He has a lovely, attractive wife, two beautiful children, and more money than he knows what to do with. But a few years ago, something happened to John that changed his life forever. While swimming alone in the ocean on a family vacation, John was hit by a huge wave and knocked unconscious. Fortunately, a little boy playing in the sand saw John's unconscious body, and got his parents to help drag the drowning man from the water. A lifeguard administered CPR, and with the care of a good doctor and the support of a loving family, John returned to health. But if you were to talk to John today, he would tell you that his life has never been the same. He says, "I wish that wave had hit me 25 years ago! I suddenly realized that my whole life needed changing. Today it is my family, my relationship to God, and what I can do for others that counts."

How long has it been since you experienced a life-changing moment like the one that changed John's life? How long has it been since something touched you so deeply that your life has never been the same? Life-changing moments like that happened to many people when they encountered Jesus Christ; Zacchaeus, about whom we read, is one of those people. On a never-to-be-forgotten-day, Zacchaeus, who looked to everyone to be a very successful person, realized that he was little more than a greedy public official who prospered by cheating others. But when he invited Jesus into his home and into his life, all that changed!

Now, do not dismiss this as a pious fairy tale, or another of those too-good-to-be-true stories they write about in *Guideposts* magazine! If you are living in a way that you are secretly ashamed of yourself, or if you have gotten away from God and the church, or if you find your days empty and meaningless, know that the Living God has a life-changing moment for you! Christianity is not just a Sunday religion we talk about in church. At the heart of the Christian faith is God's promise that you can have a new beginning, a fresh start, and a life-changing moment like that of Zacchaeus.

Look at what happened to Zacchaeus when he decided to invite Jesus Christ into his home and his life. Suddenly, Zacchaeus had a whole new understanding of himself. Everyone else in ancient Jericho knew that Zacchaeus was a liar, a loser, and a louse! Worst of all, Zacchaeus knew they were right! But along came Jesus, who would not accept the labels we or others place on our lives. Jesus treated Zacchaeus as if he were a child of God, a person of worth, and a man who still had the possibility of a new kind of life.

Zacchaeus not only changed personally, but socially as well. He came down out of that tree and, for the first time in his life, he discovered the joy of reaching out to those around him in love. In fact, the Bible says he gave away to others far beyond the value of the goods he had stolen from them. More than anything else, Zacchaeus changed in his understanding of God. Instead of thinking of God as some distant, remote judge, Zacchaeus discovered a God who offers us pardon for our past, power for our present, and promise for our future.

There is a story about a little boy who fell out of bed in the middle of the night. His mother asked him what happened, and he said, "I guess I stayed too close to where I got in!" A lot of people do that all their lives — they stay so close to where they have always been, they never discover the phenomenal power of our loving God to change our lives.

## Closing Prayer

O God, let this old story of Jesus and his love make possible a life-changing moment for us. Amen.

# 20. Handling Life's Detours

**Greeting and Call To Worship**
*Great is Thy faithfulness, O God, my Father, there is no shadow
of turning with Thee; Thou changest not; Thy compassions, they
fail not; As Thou hast been Thou forever wilt be!*

**Opening Prayer**
Faithful God, we give thanks that in a world where everything
seems to change, you remain the same yesterday, today, and forever. Help us to find our strength and our hope in you as we deal
with the changes and the frustrations we all experience. In Jesus'
precious name. Amen.

**Lord's Prayer**

**Special Hymn**                       "Great Is Thy Faithfulness"
The writer of this hymn was Thomas Obadiah Chisholm, who
was born in a log cabin near Franklin, Kentucky, in 1866. Chisholm
experienced a conversion during a revival meeting conducted by
H. C. Morrison, and moved to Louisville where he was the editor
and business manager for Morrison's *Pentecostal Herald.* Ordained
a Methodist minister at the age of 36, Chisholm became disabled.
He moved to Vineland, New Jersey, where he opened an insurance
office and worked until his retirement in 1953. During his life
Chisholm wrote more than 1,200 sacred poems. He was inspired
to write this hymn by a verse in Lamentations 3:22-23. A friend,
William M. Runyan, set it to music, and it has become a favorite
hymn of many people.

**Scripture Reading**                     Acts 16:6-10; Romans 15:22-29

**Meditation**
One of the most disheartening signs a motorist can see is the
one that says, "WARNING: DETOUR AHEAD." But detours are

more than just an inconvenience to drivers. Detours and closed roads happen in life as well. They usually take the form of disrupted plans, deferred hopes, heart-wrenching disappointments, and unrealized dreams. The Apostle Paul experienced several detours like that in his life. In the Acts of the Apostles there is a sentence about Paul's wanting to preach the gospel in a place called Bithynia. But the Bible says simply, "They were prevented from going there." Instead Paul ended up on a detour that led him to Macedonia and the continent of Europe. He wanted Bithynia, but he got Macedonia.

At the end of his Roman letter, Paul speaks about his dream of taking the Christian faith to Spain and the outermost limits of the Roman Empire. He had his heart set on it, but instead of a pulpit in Spain he ended up in a prison cell in Rome. All of us experience life's detours and the frustration of having the road before us closed. Dr. Norman Vincent Peale once had to deal with a man who complained bitterly about the problems and the obstacles that always seemed to block his way. Peale listened, and then said, "Friend, I know a place in the Bronx where there are 25,000 people with no problems!" "Oh, Norman," pleaded the man, "please take me there." "Are you sure you want to go," said Peale, "because what I have in mind is Woodlawn Cemetery!" To be alive is to face life's detours. The real question is how we handle them.

Some people handle life's frustrations and disappointments with grace and good humor. But many others become angry and bitter towards life. Still others wallow in self-pity, spending their days feeling sorry for themselves and wondering why no one finds their "pity party" very attractive. But when you study the life of the Apostle Paul, you discover a person who came to believe that with God, there is always another way. When Paul ended up in a Roman prison, his plans for carrying the message of Christ to far-off Spain blocked, he took pen in hand and began writing the Letters that comprise most of our New Testament today. Instead of giving in to frustration, Paul used the time to put his faith into words that still change lives today. He is a living example of the fact that when we hit one of life's detours, God always opens another way!

Before Abraham Lincoln became one of our greatest Presidents, he knew what it was like to have the doors of opportunity shut in his face when he failed in both business and politics. But trusting God's faithfulness, Lincoln ended up in the White House at a moment when a person of his vision, courage, and faith literally saved this nation.

Whistler, the famous painter, had planned on a career in military service. But he flunked out of West Point because he could not pass chemistry. He used to say, "If silicone had been a gas, I would have been a major general!" Only when the path he and his family had chosen was blocked did Whistler trust God to find another way.

So the message today is a very simple one. When the way is blocked for us, don't give in to anger, blame, self-pity, or despair. Our God is faithful, and with God there is always another way!

## Closing Prayer

O God, when our plans are blocked, and our dreams go unfulfilled, remind us that you are the God who is at work in everything that happens to us for good. In Jesus' name. Amen.

## Benediction

May the blessing of God Almighty, Father, Son, and Holy Spirit, be with you always. Amen.

# 21. The Prayer That Can Change Your Life

**Greeting and Call To Worship**
*Jesus said: Ask and it shall be given to you; speak and you shall find; knock and the door will be opened for you!*

**Opening Prayer**
We thank you, O God, for the gift of prayer. Forgive us when in our praying we are more concerned with ourselves than we are with the doing of your will. Teach us the importance of time spent in prayer with you each day. In the struggles and the joys of our everyday lives, remind us that you are always with us. In Jesus' name. Amen.

**Lord's Prayer**

**Special Hymn**                                         "Onward, Christian Soldiers"
This hymn was written by a busy pastor, the Reverend Sabine Baring-Gould, as a processional for singing children as they marched between villages. The author deplored its imperfections and never dreamed of its destined popularity. On one occasion, people objected to the carrying of a processional cross, so the pastor whimsically changed the last line from "with the Cross of Jesus going on before" to "with the Cross of Jesus left behind the door!" The tune for this hymn was composed by Sir Arthur Sullivan of Gilbert and Sullivan fame. The hymn reflects the fact that living the Christian life on a daily basis in an often hostile world is never easy, but it beckons us to follow the Cross of Jesus with boldness and with confidence.

**Scripture Reading**                                         Philippians 4:10-23

**Meditation**
Many years ago the great theologian Reinhold Niebuhr led the morning service in a tiny New England church. After the service,

the custodian discovered the words of a prayer Niebuhr had written for the service still on the pulpit. He was so touched by these simple words that he took the prayer and later made copies for his friends. Today almost everyone has heard the Serenity Prayer: "O God, grant me the serenity to accept the things I cannot change; the courage to change the things I can; and the wisdom to know the difference." Listening to the words Paul wrote from his prison cell to the Philippians, I suspect he must have prayed a prayer much like the Serenity Prayer many times during his confinement. Rightly understood and sincerely lived, this is without doubt a prayer that can change your life!

The first petition of this wonderful prayer asks God to give us the serenity to accept the things we cannot change. George Gallup has made a study of the things that worry us and cause us anxiety. As you might expect, finances, health problems, and the fear of accidents head the list. What is, however, even more revealing is the fact that fully 47 percent of the things most people worry about either never occur or are completely out of our control! John Watson, a theologian of long ago, wrote: "What does all your anxiety do? It does not empty tomorrow of its sorrow. Instead, it empties today of its strength. It does not make you escape the evil you fear. It only makes you unfit to cope with the evil when it comes. How different our lives would be if we stopped fretting over the things that we cannot change."

But the second petition of this famous prayer asks God to give us the courage to change the things we can. So often we become filled with hopelessness and despair because we accept the old saying, "You cannot teach an old dog new tricks." That is simply not so! When Moses was eighty years old and thinking his life was over, God called him to lead the Hebrew people out of bondage! God found a cowardly fisherman named Peter, and turned him into the leader of the early Church. God found a carnal-minded man whose life was a record of brokenness and sin, and turned him into a person we today honor as Saint Augustine. God found a woman named Ethel Waters living a sordid and wasted life, and gave her the courage to touch the hearts of the world with her music. As

Paul discovered, "I can do all things through Christ who strengthens me."

The final petition in this amazing prayer asks God for the wisdom to know the difference between the things we must accept and the things that with God's help can be changed. There is an old story about a woman staying in a fashionable Boston hotel one night. She called the manager of the hotel to complain about the noise coming from the next room where someone was playing the piano, and told him that the sound was making her dizzy and faint. The manager listened sympathetically, and then said, "I am sorry, madam, but that is the great pianist Padarewski practicing for his concert in Symphony Hall tomorrow night." "Oh my," said the unhappy woman, "that's different." The next moment she began dialing her friends in the Boston area and, before long, the famed pianist had a rapt audience listening through the wall to the music. Amazingly, the unhappy woman had made a full recovery! That's the wisdom to know the difference between what we must accept and what we can change. May this wonderful prayer change your life as it has so many of God's people.

**Closing Prayer**

O God, grant us the serenity to accept the things we cannot change; the courage to change the things we can; and the wisdom to know the difference. Amen.

**Benediction**

To God be the glory both now and forevermore. Amen.

# 22. Practice Random Acts Of Kindness

**Greeting and Call To Worship**
*O come, let us sing to God; let us make a joyful noise to the rock of our salvation! Let us come into God's presence with thanksgiving; let us make a joyful noise with songs of praise!*

**Opening Prayer**
Creator God, the whole earth proclaims your glory and shows forth the majesty of your handiwork. Even more than the world around us, we praise you today for Jesus the Christ, and your incredible gift of love and mercy to us through him. Grant us, O God, the strength and the courage we need to love one another as you have loved us. We pray in Jesus' name. Amen.

**Lord's Prayer**

**Special Hymn**                      "For The Beauty Of The Earth"
Folliott Sandford Pierpont lived from 1835 to 1917. He was born in Bath, England, and for a brief period he was headmaster and taught literature at Somersetshire College. Then, having received a small inheritance, Pierpont spent the rest of his life traveling and writing. Actually he wrote seven volumes of poems and hymns for the church! This hymn was written one day in late spring near Bath when, as Pierpont writes, "the violets and primroses were in full bloom and all the earth seemed to rejoice." The author climbed up a hill and sat down to rest and meditate. The panorama before him filled his heart with love, and inspired him to write these beautiful lines.

**Scripture Reading**       Ephesians 4:25-32; 2 Corinthians 5:16-21

**Meditation**
It all started in Sausalito, California. A woman named Anne Herbert was sitting in a restaurant when some beautiful words just

popped into her head. She jotted them down on her placemat: "Practice Random Acts of Kindness and Senseless Acts of Love." A man sitting at the next table liked those words and made a copy for himself. That's how a whole movement got started that has now swept across our whole country.

A seventh grade teacher saw these words as graffiti on a wall as she drove to work. Inspired by them, she wrote them on her classroom blackboard for her students to copy. One student took the words home. His mother, a newspaper columnist, liked them and used them in her article the next day. Before long, these few simple words, "Practice Random Acts of Kindness and Senseless Acts of Love," began appearing on billboards, bumper stickers, business cards, and refrigerators all over America. Today there is a Practice Random Acts of Kindness Week held in February each year.

What do those words mean? Simply this: help others around you with no expectations; make the world a better place by being a loving person; startle people with your acts of kindness and generosity. Here is how some people have responded: A woman in San Francisco gave the toll taker at the Golden Gate Bridge seven commuter tickets, each worth $2, and said, "This is for me and the next six drivers behind me. Have a nice day!" A teenage boy in Chicago heard these words, and got up early to shovel snow from his father's driveway. It was so much fun, he did the driveways of every other house in the neighborhood!

Now perhaps you are saying to yourself, "There's nothing so new and unique about all this. After all, two thousand years ago Jesus came to this earth to show us how to be kind and gracious, thoughtful and loving to those around us." But here is a movement that is touching human hearts and changing human lives in a way that challenges those of us who call ourselves "Christians" to really practice what we have always preached!

Every follower of Jesus is called to be an ambassador for Christ. Every one of us, by practicing acts of kindness and love each day, continues the same ministry of love Jesus began in this earthly life. We are Christ's representatives. We bear Christ's name. The Spirit of Jesus lives in our hearts when we act in a loving and gracious way to the people around us. This is the ministry given to every single person who follows Christ, and never doubt for one moment that it makes a difference.

Listen to the words of the late newsman Charles Kuralt, who traveled all over America: "To read the front pages of our papers, you might conclude that most Americans are out for themselves. The front pages have room only for cheating defense contractors and politicians with their hands in the till. But you cannot travel the back roads very long without discovering a multitude of gentle people, doing good for others with no expectation of gain or public recognition. The everyday kindness of the back roads more than makes up for the acts of greed in the headlines. There are a lot of Christians out there quietly doing what Christians have always done — loving their neighbors as Christ as loved them." Practice Random Acts of Kindness — this is a ministry for Christ in which you can share, and with God's help, you will make a difference!

**Closing Prayer**

O God, make us kind, tenderhearted, forgiving one another as God in Christ has forgiven us. Amen.

**Benediction**

May God's grace, mercy, and peace be with you always. Amen.

# 23. Afraid And Overwhelmed

**Greeting and Call To Worship**
*The Lord is my light and my salvation; whom shall I fear? The Lord is the stronghold of my life; of whom shall I be afraid?*

**Opening Prayer**
O God, our Rock, we find ourselves tossed about in the storms of life. Sometimes we become so anxious and afraid that we lose our way. In our weakness, O God, grant us power. In our fear, O God, grant us courage. We pray in the name of Jesus our Lord. Amen.

**Lord's Prayer**

**Special Hymn**                    "Guide Me, O Thou Great Jehovah"
The Welsh people may well be the most enthusiastic singers in the world. Welsh miners customarily sang on their way to the coal pits. In the great spiritual revivals which have come to Wales, music was more important than preaching. One of Wales' greatest hymn writers in the late eighteenth century was the layman-preacher William Williams. During forty years of ministry he traveled almost 100,000 miles, on foot and on horseback, preaching and singing. The best known of his 800 hymns is "Guide Me, O Thou Great Jehovah." It reminds us that we are all like pilgrims on a journey from the cradle to the grave. Along the way, our lives will sometimes seem like a "barren land." Many times, like the Hebrews of old, we will call upon God to sustain us in the moments when we feel most afraid and overwhelmed.

**Scripture Reading**                    Mark 4:35-41

**Meditation**
And Jesus said to his disciples, "Why are you afraid?" As I read that story of the terrible storm at sea, I find myself saying,

"Who wouldn't be afraid in a moment like that?" A number of years ago my family and I took a boat from Portsmouth, New Hampshire, to visit the Cornell University Marine Laboratory on Albacore Island, ten miles out to sea. The sky was almost black as we left the dock, and the fog quickly became so thick that morning you could not see any other vessels. All you could hear was the sound of boat whistles and horns as each craft tried to warn others of its presence.

There was one horn, however, that sounded through the fog louder than any other. It was somewhere off to our right, and we seemed to be on a parallel course with the other ship. Then the noise of the horn grew louder and more insistent! People on our boat lined the rails in fear and uncertainty. Suddenly, a huge Coast Guard vessel broke through the fog on a collision course with our boat! It looked so large, it was like looking up at the Queen Mary from a tiny canoe! Both captains saw the collision coming. Engines were reversed. Black smoke poured from the stacks. Water churned beneath our boat but, somehow, we managed to miss hitting the other boat by six feet! It was a terrifying experience!

Certainly, some kinds of fear can be good for us. We have learned to fear fires and earthquakes, tornadoes and floods, and we take precautions to avoid being hurt. But when an unexpected storm breaks upon us, we learn that fear can be a terrible thing. When fear strikes, the roof of our mouth goes dry. Our palms become sweaty, and terror fills our heart. Perhaps the worst thing about fear is the feeling that we are not adequate to deal with whatever it is we face. Whether it is a child who is afraid of the dark, or a soldier on a battlefield terrified of incoming shells, fear is a paralyzing experience.

From this story of Jesus and his disciples caught in the sudden unexpected storm at sea we learn several important things. First is the simple fact that trouble has a way of revealing what we are really made of. If Jesus had asked James and John and Peter on that sunny afternoon when they boarded their boat if they really trusted in God, I can imagine them saying, "Lord, you know we trust in God!" Yet, in the midst of that awful storm, even these experienced sailors feared for their lives. The storms of life have a way of testing us and forcing us to see who it is we really trust and rely on in the crisis moments.

But the even more important truth in this story is the difference the presence of Jesus makes for his disciples. The writer of the story contrasts "a great storm" with a "great calm" after Jesus spoke to the wind and the waves. Jesus' lordly presence is not a magic wand that keeps us from ever facing the storms of life, but it is enough to hold us steady when we feel afraid and overwhelmed. The poet Annie Johnson Flint has written some lines I first learned as a child about the promises of God. She writes:

> *God has not promised skies always blue,*
> *Flower-strewn pathways all our lives through;*
> *God hath not promised sun without rain, joy without*
> *      sorrow, or peace without pain.*
> *But God hath promised strength for the day,*
> *Rest for the labor and light for the way;*
> *Grace for the trials, help from above, unfailing sympa-*
> *      thy, and undying love.*

## Benediction

The grace of the Lord Jesus Christ, and the love of God, and the communion of the Holy Spirit be with you all. Amen.

# 24. Roads To Happiness

**Greeting and Call To Worship**

*The Lord is my shepherd, I shall not want. He maketh me to lie down in green pastures; he leadeth me beside the still waters; he restoreth my soul!*

**Opening Prayer**

O God, our Good Shepherd, sometimes the pathway of life is long and difficult. The burdens and heartaches of life rob us of the happiness and joy we yearn to experience. Deliver us, O God, from bitterness and despair. Remind us that the Living Christ walks beside us through every day. He is the way, the truth, and the life, and in him may we find our true joy. Amen.

**Lord's Prayer**

**Special Hymn**                                        "He Leadeth Me"

Joseph H. Gilmore, the writer of this hymn, was a Baptist minister in Philadelphia. In March of 1862, he preached a sermon based on Psalm 23, and was inspired to write this hymn text to close that service. His wife sent it to a Baptist paper, and eventually it found its way into most hymn books. The hymn writer has a vision of our lives as a journey through all sorts of experiences — hardship, ease, joy, pain, and loss. But always on that journey is the sense of Someone who goes before us, Someone who knows the way and will stretch out a helping, guiding hand whenever it is needed.

**Scripture Reading**                                        John 14:1-6

**Meditation**

It is amazing how many people live out their lives in unhappiness, bitterness, and sadness. There was a little boy trying to raise some money by collecting old bottles. He stopped at the home of a woman who was known as the "Town Grouch." "Do you have any old Coke bottles?" he asked. "No, I do not," she snapped. "Do you have any old whiskey bottles?" asked the boy. "Young man, do I look like the kind of person who would have old whiskey bottles around? Shame on you!" The boy studied her unhappy and twisted face for a moment and then asked, "Well, then, do you have any old vinegar bottles I could have?"

How sad that so many people live out their days in unhappiness when God intended our lives on this earth to be full, happy, joyous, and meaningful. But the key to happiness in this life is not clout out there in the world, but Christ living in here in our hearts. The key to happiness is not possessing a lot of things, but being possessed by the Living Christ who walks beside us each day. If Jesus is the way, then we will find the happiness and joy we yearn for by following the same roads Jesus walked in his life on earth.

Jesus changed a man's whole life on the road to Damascus. Saul, the persecutor, became Paul, the missionary to the world for Christ. Most truly happy people are those who somewhere along the way have experienced a life-changing moment. It may not be anywhere near as dramatic as Paul's experience, but it was a moment when they moved from self-centeredness to Christ-centeredness. Dr. James Simpson was a Scottish surgeon who became famous as the discoverer of anesthesia. Toward the end of his life he was asked, "What was your greatest discovery?" Without hesitation he responded, "The greatest discovery of my life is that I am a great sinner, and Jesus Christ is a great savior!" That's the same discovery Paul made on the road to Damascus.

A second road Jesus walked, and we must too, is the road to Jericho. That was the scene of Jesus' famous story about a good Samaritan who stopped to help a man who had been beaten and robbed and left by the side of the road. Jesus' whole life was spent showing the same kind of compassion and kindness that the Samaritan traveler showed to the man who had been mugged. Those who walk that same road of selfless love and concern for others have discovered a joy in their own lives that nothing can ever take away.

And then there is the other road our Lord traveled in his life — the road to Calvary. Jesus knew that almost certain death awaited

81

him when he set his face towards Jerusalem, but he traveled that road in the assurance that God would lead the way, and God would bring him through whatever he faced! The Christian's true joy is not in knowing what lies ahead, but in knowing that Christ will be there to help us face whatever comes.

## Closing Words

One night a man had a dream. He dreamed he was walking along the beach with the Lord. Scenes from his life flashed across the sky and he noticed two sets of footprints in the sand: one belonging to him and the other to the Lord. When the last scene of his life had flashed before him, he recalled that at the lowest and saddest times of his life there was only one set of footprints. Dismayed, he asked, "Lord, you said you'd walk with me all the way. Why, at the troublesome times of my life, did you leave me?" "My precious child," said the Lord, "I love you and would never leave you. During your times of trial and suffering, when you saw only one set of footprints, that was when I carried you."

# 25. Standing On The Promises

**Greeting and Call To Worship**
*The Psalmist wrote: My help cometh from the Lord who made heaven and earth. Jesus said: Lo, I am with you always, even unto the close of the age!*

**Opening Prayer**
Gracious God, you have made great promises to your people. Forgive us when we doubt them, or simply forget all that you have told us about your faithfulness and your forgiving love. May we learn to take our stand not on our own strength, but on the wondrous promises of our gracious God. Amen.

**Lord's Prayer**

**Special Hymn**                    "My Hope Is Built On Nothing Less"
The text of this hymn was written by Edward Mote. The idea came to him as he was preparing to visit the bedside of a dying parishioner. He shared these words with the dying man, and they meant so much to him that Mote published them in a leaflet in his church. Mote was born in London, where his parents owned a pub. According to him, his parents were not God-fearing people. At age sixteen, he was working as a cabinetmaker when his employer took him to an evangelistic service. There he gave his heart to Christ, and made the decision to become a Baptist pastor.

**Scripture Reading**                    John 14:8-17, 25-27

**Meditation**
The Bible is a book filled with promises from God to help us live richer and fuller lives on this earth and for eternity. But how important are those promises in our everyday lives? I have a book in my library titled *Are You Standing On The Promises, Or Just Sitting On The Premises?* The question is, do you in your heart

embrace the great promises of God, or are you just sitting listlessly on the sidelines, letting these words go in one ear and out the other?

One of the problems we face as we get older is that we forget those things we ought to remember. A husband and wife discovered a new restaurant, and they just loved it! The next evening they had some friends over to their house, and while the wife was out in the kitchen fixing coffee, the husband began telling about this wonderful new restaurant. "It sounds wonderful," said the friends, "but what is the name of the restaurant?" The husband could not remember the name. Then he said, "Wait, I have an idea. What is that flower that has a long stem, a beautiful blossom, and thorns?" "A rose," suggested the friends. "That's it!" said the husband excitedly. Turning towards the kitchen, he shouted, "Hey, Rose, will you come in here and tell us the name of the restaurant we liked so much last night?"

Now that is forgetfulness! But Jesus must have known how human it is to forget. On that night when he met with his disciples in the Upper Room just before his death, he repeated one of his greatest promises no less than five times! It was the promise, "I will not leave you alone ... I will be with you ... even to the end of the world!" If that great promise does not excite you, thrill you, and encourage you, you need to check your pulse or have someone see if you are still breathing!

This is God's promise to comfort us in the rough places in our lives. That word "comfort" literally means "with strength." People who are comforted by God are given a strength greater than their own to face the tough times. Back in the 1950s the name Ted Husing was a household word for anyone who listened to the radio. Ted was a very popular announcer at the peak of his career when he had to undergo a brain operation that left him paralyzed, blind, and unable to speak. He became bitter and discouraged, and would not even see his friends. But some of his Christian friends would not take "No" for an answer. They made him go with them to a baseball game where Ted could hear the crack of the bat and smell the hot dogs and peanuts. Then a friend said to him, "Ted, you are going to get through this. People all over this country are praying for you and they seem to know something you have forgotten — that God has promised to be with you all the way." Ted Husing later wrote that it was this reminder of God's comforting presence that turned his life around.

The other great truth in this promise of Christ is that God will give us not only comfort, but courage. All of us need the courage to act when we are afraid; the courage to stand up for the truth when it is so easy to remain silent; the courage to help someone in need when it is so easy just to turn our heads the other way. One day an American visiting as a tourist in the Middle East saw a man on a bicycle, balancing a basket of oranges, crash into a porter who was carrying a heavy burden on his shoulder. The two were about to come to blows when, suddenly, the American tourist stepped between them and kissed the clenched fists of both men. The crowd applauded, and, eventually, the two men involved in the accident ended up hugging each other. Someone said to the American, "Where did you get the courage to do what you did?" His answer was simply, "The Spirit of Jesus gave me the courage to be a peacemaker!"

**Closing Prayer**

O God, teach us once more how important it is to stand on the solid rock of your promises to us. Amen.

# 26. Turning Inkblots Into Angels

**Greeting and Call To Worship**
*In this the love of God was made manifest among us, that God sent the only Son into the world, so that we might live through him!*

**Opening Prayer**
Eternal God, your love is like a light in the midst of this world's darkness. Pardon our sin, and give us such joy in Jesus Christ that darkness may be driven from our lives and your light will shine forth in us. We pray in the name of Christ our Lord. Amen.

**Lord's Prayer**

**Special Hymn** "Dear Lord And Father Of Mankind"
John Greenleaf Whittier, the "Quaker poet," was born in Haverhill, Massachusetts, in 1807. He began life as a farm boy and then became a village shoemaker. With only a meager education, he entered the field of journalism and eventually held editorial positions in Boston, Hartford, and Philadelphia. He was an ardent opponent of slavery, and used his skills as a writer to work for its abolition. Eventually he was recognized as one of America's great poets, and over fifty hymns in modern use found their inspiration in his beautiful poems. The melody by Frederick Charles Maker is the perfect setting for the Quaker poet's prayerful words.

**Scripture Reading** Romans 8:28-39

**Meditation**
From Scotland comes the story of Joseph Craik, who became known all over that land as the man who could turn inkblots into angels. Craik was a talented penman and artist. He was appointed "writing master" in a village school back in the days when students learned to write by dipping their pens into inkwells. If you

recall, most of us ended up turning in papers to our teacher with unwanted inkblots all over them! Most teachers in that school circled the inkblots on the student's papers in large red circles. But Craik, instead of chastising his students for their mistakes, would add a line here and there to their inkblots so that they became pictures of angels. As you can imagine, Joseph Craik became a legend in his own time as the "man who could turn inkblots into angels."

That story is a wonderful parable of the difference Christian faith can make in a person's life. By the miracle of grace, God turns the inkblots and mistakes in our lives into something good. God takes our feeble efforts and uses them for good in a way we never thought possible. That is precisely what Paul was saying in this magnificent portion of his Roman Letter: "We know that in everything, God is at work for good ... nothing shall ever separate us from the love of God in Christ Jesus our Lord!" Let me remind you that the person who wrote those words was no television talk-show host handing out easy advice. Paul knew firsthand about hardship, disappointment, rejection, physical pain, and chronic illness. But Paul discovered in Christ someone whose power could transform the inkblots in his life into angels.

God is still ready to transform our despair into hope. In those moments of life where we hurt the most, the God who is at work for good in everything that happens to us is still able to turn dark inkblots into angels of hope. Author Frederick Buechner was at a low point in his life. He was worried to death about his daughter, who was ill, and was so weighed down with despair that he questioned the very existence of God. One day while driving his car his eyes filled with tears, and he had to pull to the side of the road. As he sat there crying, "God, where are you?" a car came toward him with one of those personalized license plates on the front. On the license plate was the single word "TRUST." For Buechner, it was one of those transforming moments when his doubt was overcome, his trust in God renewed, and his life turned around. He later learned that the license plate belonged to the Trust Officer of his local bank! But isn't that exactly how God works to turn inkblots into angels in our everyday lives?

Sometimes God turns our problems into opportunities. Back in 1850 a young man from Bavaria came to this country to get in on the gold rush in our Western states. He carried with him rolls of canvas which he believed could be made into tents for the miners traveling westward in search of gold. But to his dismay, the miners did not want tents! They said to him, "What we really need are pants — durable pants that can stand up to the rough life of a miner." So this young man from Bavaria decided to turn his rolls of canvas into blue pants that could survive the rigors of the mining camps. He got a harness-maker to reinforce the pockets with copper studs, and his pants became an overnight success! In case you haven't guessed, the name of the young man from Bavaria was Levi Strauss, and his pants, called "Levi's," have been selling in basically their original form for the last 130 years!

Inkblots into angels — the God we meet in Jesus Christ is a God whose love will never let us go. This is a God who is at work in everything that happens to us for good.

**Closing Prayer**

"Dear Lord and Father of mankind, forgive our foolish ways; Reclothe us in our rightful mind, in purer lives Thy service find, in deeper reverence, praise."

# 27. The Healing Power Of Love

**Greeting and Call To Worship**
*God so loved the world that God sent the only begotten Son, so that all who believe in Him should not perish, but have everlasting life!*

**Opening Prayer**
Gracious God, we give thanks for the gift of your amazing love in Jesus Christ. We stand in awe of the fact that while we were yet sinners, Christ died for us! O God, teach us not only to be thankful for this love we will never deserve, but to be courageous enough to love others in the same incredible way you have loved us. Amen.

**Lord's Prayer**

**Special Hymn**                    "Jesus Loves Me"
The text of this familiar hymn was written by Anna Bartlett Warner for her novel, *Say And Seal*, in 1859. The main characters of this novel were a dying child, Johnny Fax, and his Sunday School teacher, John Linden. Toward the end of the story, the teacher, John Linden, carried the child and sang to him what has now become the familiar children's hymn. Anna Warner and her sister Susan, daughters of a New York lawyer, between them wrote more than seventy books. Every Sunday afternoon in their home near West Point, they taught a Bible class to the cadets. The sisters were buried with full military honors in recognition of the contribution they made to the lives of young military officers.

**Scripture Reading**                    John 15:12-17

**Meditation**

A young mother was coming out of the grocery store accompanied by four small, lively children, and pushing a cart that was loaded with purchases. An older man watched for a moment and then said, "How do you ever manage to divide your love among those four active children?" The young mother looked up and, with a smile, she said, "I don't divide it ... I multiply it!"

There is nothing in this world more powerful than love. Sometimes we forget just how powerful love is. The world keeps asking us to put our trust in military might, economic strength, and political clout, but it is love that makes the world go around. The Bible insists that love is the single most authentic sign of a person being Christ's disciple. On that last night of his earthly life, gathered with his disciples in the Upper Room, Jesus kept talking about love. "This is my commandment, that you love one another as I have loved you." Jesus could have spent that night reviewing the Ten Commandments, or describing in detail what heaven will be like, but he didn't! Instead, the Great Physician talked about the incredible power of love to heal our broken lives. The famous psychiatrist Karl Menninger once said, "There is nothing worse, and nothing more devastating in human experience, than the feeling of being unloved. On the other hand, love has the power to cure, both the ones who give it and the ones who receive it."

Jesus knows that love has the power to heal us physically. That does not mean that love is a substitute for a good doctor, but unconditional love like that of Jesus Christ can play a big part in the healing process. A woman in Sweden was taken to a rehabilitation center following a mild stroke. She was a very difficult patient, because she had not spoken for weeks. A Christian nurse, who believed that real love is not an emotion but rather an act of the will, decided to love this difficult patient with the unconditional love she had seen in Christ. Instead of shouting at the patient or ignoring her, she pulled up a rocker next to the rocker of her patient. They sat there together, and occasionally the nurse would reach over and pat the hands of the patient. This went on for a week when, suddenly, the older woman turned to the nurse and said, "You are very kind." A few days later, she began talking normally and, after several months, the patient was able to return to her home.

Now it does not always work out so wonderfully as that, but do not miss the incredible power of love to heal us and make us whole physically. Love also has incredible power to heal the emotional and spiritual hurts in our lives as well. Often beneath our outwardly smiling faces there exist deep scars from painful hurts. It may be the memory of a child rushing downstairs to open a Christmas stocking and finding instead a lump of coal as punishment for some trivial childhood naughtiness. Or it may be the painful memory of someone who introduced us to the mysteries of sex long before we were ready for that relationship. It may be an ancient guilt that haunts us day and night.

Those are the kinds of hurts that can only be healed by the awesome power of God's love. A young woman named Nancy felt a desperate need to be loved. So low was her self-esteem and so great was her need that she would give herself to whatever man she was with. In the small town where Nancy lived, she became a "woman with a reputation." Then one day Nancy met a Christian man who fell deeply in love with her. He knew all about her past, but together they began to pray for God's healing in her life. Nancy became a beautiful, radiant woman, the living proof of the healing power of God's love!

### Closing Prayer

O God, heal us with the amazing power of your love in Christ Jesus our Lord. Amen.

# 28. Staying Alive As Long As You Live

**Greeting and Call To Worship**
*Jesus said: I am the bread of life. Whoever comes to me will never be hungry, and whoever believes in me will never be thirsty.*

**Opening Prayer**
O God of abundant life, forgive us when we let our days and years become nothing more than routine existence. Show us how to live the abundant life Jesus intends for us, regardless of age. Make our days special and our years meaningful through the grace of Jesus Christ our Lord. Amen.

**Lord's Prayer**

**Special Hymn**         "Have Thine Own Way, Lord"
As she sat in a prayer meeting one night, Adelaide Pollard, the writer of this hymn, was so depressed that she could hardly concentrate on what was being said. She had felt a heavy burden on her heart for Africa, and was convinced that God wanted her to go there as a missionary. She was ready to set sail aboard a ship, but the necessary funds could not be raised and her trip was canceled. After returning home that evening, Adelaide Pollard meditated on the story of the potter in Jeremiah 18:3-4. She was a gifted teacher of the Bible and a talented writer. She had a real passion for missions, but it seemed as if God had other plans for her. As she thought about the potter breaking the defective vessel, she wrote, "It's all right, Lord! It doesn't matter what you bring into our lives; just have your own way with us!" From those few lines has come this hymn which has touched so many hearts.

**Scripture Reading**         Romans 12:3-18

## Meditation

There were three clergypersons discussing the issue of when human life actually begins. "Life begins at the moment of conception!" said the Catholic priest. "No, no," said the Presbyterian pastor, "life begins at the moment of birth." The third clergyperson was an aging rabbi who said thoughtfully, "You're both wrong! Life really begins when the dog dies and the children leave home!" When does real "living" begin?

The Apostle Paul was convinced that Jesus had come to this earth to bring us "abundant life." That is, life with a capital "L." For Paul, this was a life that could begin at any age when people put their trust in Christ. It was a life filled with a lilt and a luster that not even years could take away. Writing in the 12th Chapter of Romans, Paul is talking about what it takes to stay alive as long as you live.

He begins by saying the abundant life in Christ gives you a sense of worth that nothing can take away. Says Paul, "Don't cherish exaggerated ideas of your own importance ... but try to have a sane estimate of your capabilities by the light of faith God has given you." So often our culture determines the worth of persons by how much money they make, or how much they can achieve. At a Christmas party given for former employees of a large corporation, a bright young woman was welcoming the guests who were the retired officers of that company. She walked up to one man and asked, "And who did you used to be?" It was as if that retired man no longer had value or worth simply because he was no longer working!

The Apostle Paul wanted his friends in Rome to know that our personal worth is not based on our accomplishments, nor our power or prestige, nor the size of our bank account, nor even our age. When people put their trust in Jesus Christ, they become people loved and precious in the sight of God! They become persons for whom the Son of God poured out his life on a Cross.

Then Paul goes on to say that the abundant life in Christ gives us another essential for staying alive as long as we live: a sense of purpose. Having a purpose is what makes life worthwhile. Helen Keller once said that she wanted to do more than "spend" her life

93

— she wanted to "invest" it! Jesus Christ offers each of us the chance to invest our lives in the greatest purpose of all time — the bringing of God's Kingdom to this earth. No matter how old or how infirm we may be, there is always something we can do for Jesus Christ! Many people think they have no gift that Christ can use. But someone once said, "It is amazing how much God can accomplish through an imperfect person who is willing to put all of his or her imperfections at God's disposal."

Still a third ingredient for staying alive as long as you live, according to Paul, is a positive mental outlook. Paul says, "Base your happiness on your hope in Christ." That is, do not focus on your problems but instead keep your eyes on the Living Christ. An old hymn carries the same message: "Turn your eyes upon Jesus; look full in his wonderful face. And the things of earth will grow strangely dim, in the light of his glory and grace." With our eyes on Christ, every day can be a new experience of abundant life!

**Closing Prayer**

O God, fill us with your Spirit, so that we can live our lives in the fullness of your joy and in the knowledge that we are precious in your sight. In Jesus' name we pray. Amen.

# 29. Here's Jesus! (Advent)

**Greeting and Call To Worship**
*God so loved the world that God sent the only begotten Son, so that all who believe in him should not perish, but have everlasting life!*

**Opening Prayer**
Lord Jesus Christ, we praise you for bringing to us the gift of God's mercy and forgiveness. We give thanks that you came to this earth to live the same life we experience each day, and to know its joys and its heartaches. Even more, we are grateful that the Risen Christ is our daily companion. Be present with us now in our worship, and to you be all glory. Amen.

**Lord's Prayer**

**Special Hymn**                                      "Fairest Lord Jesus"
The origin of this hymn is somewhat difficult to trace. One tradition says that it was first called the "Crusaders' Hymn" because it was said to have been sung by the German knights on their way to Jerusalem during the Crusades. Most scholars, however, believe that this hymn was originally a folk song sung by the people in the district of Glaz, in Lower Silesia. A final stanza that begins "Beautiful Savior, Lord of the nations" was added by a Lutheran pastor, Joseph Seiss, from Philadelphia. Whatever its origins, this hymn is a wonderful tribute to the Lordship of Christ.

**Scripture Reading**                                  Philippians 2:5-11

**Meditation**
During a children's sermon, a pastor asked the children, "What is gray, has a bushy tail, and gathers nuts in the fall?" One little boy raised his hand and said, "I know the answer should be 'Jesus,'

but it sounds an awful lot like a squirrel to me!" That little fellow sitting in church knew that Christianity is Jesus Christ! In the Philippian Letter, Paul has written one of the most beautiful hymns of praise to Jesus. Do you recall how on the *Tonight Show* for many years, when he introduced Johnny Carson, the announcer would say, "H-E-E-E-R-E'S Johnny?" In like manner Paul is saying to us, "H-E-E-E-R-E'S Jesus!" But just what does Jesus mean to the Christian?

Paul speaks first about the Christ Who Is Above Us. Jesus is more than a good person; Jesus is the Lord of heaven and earth. He is God in human flesh and there is no one quite like him. Until recently there was a rule in Philadelphia that no building could go higher than the hat on the statue of William Penn. That's how a Christian thinks of Jesus. Jesus is our model for life on earth. Jesus is the Savior who died on the Cross for our sins. Jesus is the one through whom we pray to God, and Jesus is the Lord of life to whom we surrender our hearts.

But Paul also wants us to ponder the mystery of Christ In Us. A Christian is someone in whom the Spirit of Jesus lives today. Paul in his many letters uses the phrase "in Christ" at least 164 times. That is not mere poetic language. It is living so close to Jesus that we gradually become like Jesus. It was said of Saint Francis that he lived so closely to Jesus that eventually people could see in Francis' hands the same nail prints that were in Christ's hands on the Cross.

The world sometimes doubts this sense of the Living Christ's presence with us. A little boy spilled some milk at the dinner table and his mother told him to go out on the back porch and get the floor mop. He went to the back door and looked out. It was very dark and he was frightened. His mother said, "Don't be afraid; Jesus is with you." The little boy opened the door and said, "Jesus, if you're really out there, would you please hand me the mop!" We understand that little boy's dilemma, but down through the ages Christians have experienced that wonderful sense of Christ's Presence within us.

Paul adds one more dimension to his understanding of Jesus — the Christ Beyond Us. Jesus goes before us like a good shepherd.

There is nothing we will face in this life or the next that Christ has not already experienced. He is the pioneer of our faith journey, the one who goes before us to show us the way to a right relationship with God. A little boy was watching a parade when President Theodore Roosevelt passed by riding on his horse. The little boy took off his hat and said to his parents, "Someday, I want to be like him." That's how a Christian feels about Jesus Christ!

## Closing Prayer

Lord, help us through the power of your Holy Spirit to become more like Jesus every day. Surround us with the assurance of your love and your presence with us, not only today, but always. We pray in Jesus' name. Amen.

## Benediction

The Lord bless you and keep you. The Lord make God's face to shine upon you and be gracious to you. The Lord lift up God's countenance upon you and give you peace, both now and forevermore. Amen.

# 30. A Light Shines In The Darkness (Christmas)

**Greeting and Call To Worship**

*Behold, I bring you good tidings of great joy! For unto you is born this day, in the City of David, a Savior who is Christ the Lord!*

**Opening Prayer**

O God, as we gather in your presence this day, may our hearts catch the wonder and the glory that the Word of God has become flesh and dwelt among us. May we rejoice this day that your light has entered our world, and the darkness will never overcome it. Fill us with your Living Spirit, so that the light of your love may shine forth to the world through us. In Jesus' name. Amen.

**Lord's Prayer**

**Special Hymn**            "O Little Town Of Bethlehem"

The words to this familiar carol were written by the Reverend Phillips Brooks, who at the time was pastor of Holy Trinity Episcopal Church in Philadelphia. Several years before writing this hymn, Brooks had spent Christmas Eve traveling to Bethlehem on horseback so that he could worship in the Church of the Nativity. No doubt his experience then inspired the writing of this carol in 1868 for the Christmas Sunday School program. The music for this carol was composed by Lewis Henry Redner, who was the organist and choir director at the church where Brooks was pastor. Brooks asked Redner to compose a melody simple enough for children to sing. The melody finally came to Redner during the night on the Saturday before the program, and he finished composing the harmony before going to church on Sunday.

**Scripture Reading**                                      John 1:1-14

**Meditation**

Some of the deepest truths of the Bible are communicated to us in metaphors — figures of speech that light up a truth in a way everybody can understand. Jesus talked about sheep and shepherds, seeds and a sower, a lost coin and a lost boy. Sometimes metaphors bring a smile to our faces. I have heard pastors who are too busy in their work described as "dogs at a whistlers' convention." A rather crotchety old man was described by a friend as "someone who was weaned on a dill pickle." These figures of speech help us to understand a deeper truth.

In John's Gospel, the story of Christ's birth is told using the metaphors of light and darkness. John tells us: "The light shines in the darkness, and the darkness has not overcome it." Think for a moment of the contrast between light and darkness in the familiar story: There is darkness over Bethlehem until an incredibly bright star appears in the heavens. Out on the dark Judean hillsides, the shepherds are suddenly awakened by a bright light and the singing of angels.

Light is the most stable reality in our universe. It is the standard by which we measure the speed of most things. It is the essential ingredient that makes life on this earth possible. We see its beauty in the rainbow, and its power in the laser beam. When John uses this image of light, he wants us to think about the incredible love of God for this dark, broken, sinful world. The other great faiths of the world present a God who loves people, but that love is conditioned by people obeying God's rules, or performing acts that make them pleasing to the deity. Only Christianity dares us to believe in a God whose love reaches out to us when we are unlovable, or when life has turned sour. Only Christianity dares us to believe in a God who comes seeking us out in all the places where we hide.

But John not only wants us to think about the wonder of a God who comes as a light into our darkness. He wants us also to recognize that the light is powerful enough to transform our lives, and the darkness in which much of our world lives. Wally Purling was nine years old and in the second grade. He was big for his age, clumsy, and had a hard time keeping up with the other children. As Christmas drew near, the town got ready for the annual nativity play, and Wally wanted more than anything to have a part. Because of his size, the director asked Wally to play the part of the innkeeper who turned Mary and Joseph away. There were few lines to memorize.

On the night of the performance, no one was more excited than Wally Purling. He waited his turn anxiously, and then opened the door to the inn. Joseph pleaded for a place to stay, but Wally, looking properly stern, said his line: "Seek lodging elsewhere. The inn is full." Joseph pleaded with the innkeeper, "Sir, my wife is heavy with child. Surely you must have some small corner where she can rest." There was a long, uncomfortable silence as Wally stood there looking at Joseph and Mary. The prompters off stage whispered Wally's line, "No, begone!" Suddenly as Wally Purling's eyes filled with tears, this Christmas pageant became different from all others. Just as Joseph and Mary turned away, Wally the innkeeper shouted, "Mary, Joseph, come on back! You can have my room in the inn tonight!" Some thought the Christmas program had been ruined, but others felt it just might be the most Christ-like Christmas pageant they had ever seen. For the miracle of God's love opened a little boy's heart, and once more, the light transformed the darkness of our world.

### Closing Prayer

"O Holy Child of Bethlehem, descend to us, we pray. Cast out our sin and enter in, be born in us today."

# 31. So, What's New? (New Year)

**Greeting and Call To Worship**

*Before the mountains were brought forth or ever you had formed the earth and the world, even from everlasting to everlasting, you are God!*

**Opening Prayer**

Eternal and Unchanging God, let the light of your presence shine on us today, making plain some answers to our questions, some assurance for our doubts, and some strength for our weakness. We confess the failures of our past, and we bring to you our hopes for this New Year. Draw near to us as we draw near to you. Amen.

**Lord's Prayer**

**Special Hymn**                                    "Hark! The Herald Angels Sing"

The words to this familiar carol were written by the great Methodist hymn writer, Charles Wesley. The original poem began, "Hark, how all the welkin rings, Glory to the King of kings." "Welkin" was an archaic word that meant "heavens" or "sky." Fourteen years later, Wesley changed this hymn to "Hark! The herald angels sing" to capture the glory and the joy of that first Christmas morning. The melody was written by the great composer Felix Mendelssohn. At 17, he composed his overture to *A Midsummer Night's Dream*. The melody for this carol was taken unaltered from the second movement of that composition.

**Scripture Reading**                              Jeremiah 31:7-14

**Meditation**

How often when you meet someone does he or she say to you, "So, what's new with you?" And often we respond, "Oh, nothing much, really. How 'bout you?" But I cannot help wondering what would happen if we Christians here at the beginning of the New Year had the courage to say: "I'll tell you what's new — it's the good news of what God has done for this world in Jesus Christ!" Wouldn't that be a startling change from the hackneyed "Happy New Year," or even the clever greeting a friend once gave me: "Pastor, may all your troubles last as long as your New Year's resolutions!"

So what is new about what God has done for this world in sending the Messiah, Jesus the Christ? Long before Jesus ever walked this earth, God's prophet Jeremiah had an inspired vision of a totally new age when the Messiah would come and God's Kingdom would be established on this earth.

Jeremiah envisioned that the Messiah's coming would mean a whole new beginning for those who trusted in the salvation the Christ would bring. This was no empty promise, such as "look on the bright side of things in the new year." There was a little boy who went to his first Little League baseball practice. His father asked how he made out, and he said, "The coach says I'm the best of the worst three!" That's having a positive attitude, but Jeremiah envisions something far more radical — a complete change, a fresh start, a whole new beginning for those who will put their trust in God's redemption in Jesus Christ.

Jim was a business executive who up until a year ago had very little time for God or for the church. His career was all that mattered in his life. But knowing that he was missing something, he accepted a friend's suggestion to join him in a six-week study of the Bible during Lent. The group met each week for prayer and study, and Jim found he enjoyed the meetings. Then, on the last night together, the leader of the Bible study asked the group to share anything new in their lives as a result of their time together. To his own amazement, Jim found himself saying, "I am forgiven!" Tears began to flow down his cheeks as he added, "I know in my heart that Christ has forgiven me! I'm not the same person I was six weeks ago! I have a whole new life ahead of me!" What's new? Jeremiah says when the Messiah comes, people like us can have a whole new beginning.

More than that, Jeremiah envisioned not only a new start, but a whole new life in Christ. It is not just that in Christ God wipes the slate clean of our sinful past. In Christ, we can begin living in a whole new way — in the way of love, truth, righteousness, peace, and justice. The Holy Spirit will help us become new people who live in a whole new way! I once was given a T-shirt that had a picture on it of an apple with a bite taken out of it. Above the apple was written, "Not Perfect." Below the apple were the words, "Just Forgiven." There is little question about our being "not perfect." That is your story and mine. But we are more in Christ than "just forgiven." In Christ we are new people, forgiven and renewed in a way that we can begin living a whole new life each day. That's good news — probably the best news this old world has had for a very long time!

So when someone asks you, "What's new," next time why don't you tell the good news: In Jesus Christ, we can become a whole new person!

## Closing Prayer

God of amazing grace, remind us afresh at the beginning of this new year that in Christ we can become new men and women, and that it is not too late to make real changes in our lives. In Jesus' name. Amen.

## Benediction

The grace of the Lord Jesus Christ be with you all.

# 32. God's Surprising Presence (Epiphany)

**Greeting and Call To Worship**
*The Lord is my light and my salvation! Jesus said: "I am the light of the world." God is light, and in God is no darkness at all!*

**Opening Prayer**
God of light, we find ourselves living in a world that often seems to be filled with darkness. Sometimes we, in despair, wonder where you are in the midst of so much violence and hatred and greed. O God, remind us today that you are always with us, even in some of the most surprising places in our lives. We pray in Jesus' name. Amen.

**Lord's Prayer**

**Special Hymn**                    "Immortal, Invisible, God Only Wise"
Walter Chalmers Smith, the writer of this hymn, lived from 1824 until 1908. He was born in Aberdeen, Scotland, and was ordained to the ministry in 1850. He served churches in London, Glasgow, and Edinburgh, and became the Moderator of the Free Church of Scotland. In this beautiful hymn, God is often compared to the sun in the heavens. Like the sun, God needs nothing for sustenance; instead, all things depend upon God. God's power never diminishes, and God remains the same day in and day out.

**Scripture Reading**                    Genesis 28:10-17

**Meditation**
If someone were to ask us where the Living God is to be found, most of us would probably say in the worship of the church, in the stories of the Bible, in a quiet moment of prayer, or in the beauty of a sunrise or sunset. But the words we just read about Jacob suggest that God is often found in the most surprising and unexpected places

104

in our lives. And when we find God in those unexpected places, suddenly everything in our lives is different!

There was a young man who decided one summer while in college to work on a Texas ranch. In the springtime, it had seemed like a great way to spend a summer. But when his folks drove him out to the ranch, it was so disappointing and disillusioning. It wasn't anything like he imagined. The ranch was located way back in the hills, cut off from civilization, and a good 75 miles from the nearest Dairy Queen! Those first few days on the ranch, the young man cried himself to sleep. But then his parents noticed a sudden change in the tone of his letters. It seems the rancher's beautiful daughter had come home for the summer! Soon the young man was describing the ranch as "the most beautiful place I have ever been"! By September, the boy's parents could hardly get him back to college!

That young man found something so good in an unexpected place that it changed his whole outlook on life. As I read the Bible, I find its pages full of people who discovered the Living God in the most surprising places in their lives. Here's 80-year-old Moses who discovers God's presence in a burning bush. Here's the prophet Isaiah who discovers God while he is in captivity in Babylon. Here is Job discovering God in the midst of his pain and suffering. And here is Saul of Tarsus who meets the Risen Christ while engaged in a mission to persecute Christians!

Jacob, too, is a person who finds God in the most unexpected place. You may remember that Jacob, through deceit, lies, trickery, and connivance, literally has robbed his brother of his rightful inheritance. Weighed down with fear and guilt, Jacob is running for his life. God is the last person in the world he expects to meet out there in the wilderness, but suddenly God is there and Jacob knows that his life will never be the same again. He says, "Surely, the Lord is in this place, and I did not know it."

The simple truth is that God often comes to us when we least expect it. Here's God ministering to Jacob in the midst of one of the most anxious and stressful times in his life. Sometimes people meet the Living God in the unexpected place of sorrow in their lives. The truth is, God is never closer to us than when we are hurting. A man was sitting in his car at an intersection when another automobile turned onto his street and sideswiped his back left fender. The man got out of his car to exchange insurance information, and discovered that the driver of the other automobile was a young woman who was crying hysterically. Between sobs, she explained that she had just gotten married. The car was a wedding present from her husband, and she had never been in an accident before. She could not even move to get out her insurance card, so the man reached into the glove compartment for it. To the amazement of both, there was a note from the young woman's husband, attached to the insurance card. The note completely changed the day — it read, "Honey, in case of an accident, remember that I love you a lot more than this car!"

Sometimes in those moments of sorrow and disappointment, it is as if God sends us a note that says, "In case of a broken heart, remember I love you and will see you through!" Let's never forget to look for God in the most surprising and unexpected places in our lives.

### Benediction
May God bless you and keep you, both now and forevermore.

# 33. Yes And No
# (Lent)

**Greeting and Call To Worship**
*Stand, therefore, having your loins girded with truth, and having on the breastplate of righteousness!*

**Opening Prayer**
O God of compassion, we turn to you in the midst of a world that often wants its own will done instead of your will. Daily we are challenged in our walk of faith with the Living Christ. Fill us with your Holy Spirit, that we may act with boldness in serving Christ Jesus our Lord. Amen.

**Lord's Prayer**

**Special Hymn**                               "Stand Up, Stand Up For Jesus"
The author of this hymn, George Duffield, was inspired to write these stirring words in response to the death of a close friend, Dudley Tyng. Tyng had been a young pastor in Philadelphia in 1858. He was such an effective preacher that at a revival in Philadelphia, he once had 1,000 people give their hearts to Christ. A few weeks after this revival, Tyng was watching a cornshelling machine when his arm caught in the machinery and was terribly mangled. Friends gathered around Tyng's bed as he lay dying. Someone asked, "Dudley, do you have any last message for your friends?" "Tell them to stand up for Jesus!" George Duffield was so touched by this message that he wrote the words we will now sing.

**Scripture Reading**                               Matthew 4:1-11

**Meditation**
Consider the importance of two little words we use every day of our lives — "yes" and "no." Those two words, more than any others we speak, define our lives and what is of true importance to

us. The season of Lent is a good time to take a fresh look at the things to which we say "yes" and the things to which we say "no."

Sometimes it is a lot harder to say "no," because we want to get along with those around us or to please our friends. Think of the courage of those who said "no" to the Nazis and Adolf Hitler in Germany in the 1930s, or those with Dr. Martin Luther King, Jr., in this country who said "no" to racial segregation in the 1960s. Saying "no" is very hard for many of our young athletes as they sacrifice education for big bucks. Saying "no" to drugs and alcohol has become one of the most serious problems our teenagers face. Today one out of every twelve teenagers will have a problem with alcohol! In the business world, it is often very hard to say "no" to insider trading, crooked dealing, and unethical practices.

But when we turn to the Bible, we discover that saying "no" has never been easy for God's people. Way back in Genesis, Adam and Eve could have said "no" to the temptation to eat the forbidden fruit, and human history might be a very different story. The book of Genesis also tells the story of Joseph, who as a handsome young Hebrew man caught the eye of Potiphar's wife. Joseph was a slave in Potiphar's house, but when the Master of the House was away, his wife did everything she could to lure the handsome young Hebrew slave to her bedroom. But Joseph said "no" because "my God will see us!"

Moses said an emphatic "no" when he came down from Mount Sinai with the Ten Commandments and found the people worshipping a golden calf instead of the Living God. His hurling the two tablets at the idol was his way of saying for God, "You shall have no other gods before me!" And then here is Jesus in the wilderness just before beginning his public ministry. He is tempted to become the kind of Messiah that uses spectacular tricks to get public attention. But summoning the power of heaven to help him, Jesus says "no" to Satan and to doing things according to his will instead of God's will.

Saying "no" in the Christian life is never easy. However, saying "yes" is also very important. Traditionally, we have thought of Lent as a time to say "no" to chocolate or to ice cream — a time to deny ourselves some pleasure. Let me suggest, however, that Lent could be a wonderful time to say "yes."

Let us say "no" to grumbling and complaining, and "yes" to giving thanks to God in all circumstances. Let us say "no" to worries and fears, and "yes" to trusting God more every day. Let us say "no" to some television program, and "yes" to spending the time with someone who is lonely. Let us say "no" to that ugly bit of gossip we have heard, and "yes" to praying for those who have hurt us. God give us the courage to say "no" to the things of this world, and "yes" to the things of Jesus Christ!

## Closing Prayer

An old hymn offers a wonderful prayer for each believer:

> *I would be true, for there are those who trust me.*
> *I would be pure, for there are those who care.*
> *I would be strong, for there is much to suffer.*
> *I would be brave, for there is much to dare.*

## Benediction

May God bless you and keep you. May God's face shine on you and be gracious to you. May God look upon you with favor and give you peace.

# 34. Lost And Found
# (Lent)

**Greeting and Call To Worship**
*Jesus said: I have come to seek and to save the lost. There will be more joy in heaven over one sinner who repents than over ninety-nine righteous persons who need no repentance!*

**Opening Prayer**
God of grace and forgiveness, we come to you like the prodigal son to his father, knowing that we have no righteousness within ourselves and trusting in your mercy to restore us to your family. Cleanse our lives, and renew our spirits that we may once more be the sons and daughters of the Living God. In Jesus' name. Amen.

**Lord's Prayer**

**Special Hymn**                  "Make Me A Captive, Lord"
The opening line of this hymn may at first seem very puzzling: "Make me a captive, Lord, and then I shall be free." How can one be a captive and yet be free? George Matheson, the writer of this hymn, is describing something important that happened to him in his life. Matheson was a brilliant young theologian with a promising career as a Christian scholar. But as a young man, he lost his eyesight completely. It meant giving up his love of research and scholarship. However, George Matheson said, "When I became blind, I really began to see." What he meant by that was that in his utter dependence on God, he learned to read the hearts of people and to live closer to God than ever before.

**Scripture Reading**                            Luke 15:1-24

**Meditation**
Can you think back to a time in your life when you were lost? I am sure you would agree that being lost is a terrible experience.

As a boy, I was attending a county fair one evening when I became separated from my parents. I stopped to look at something and, the next moment, I realized that nothing around me looked familiar. Fighting back the tears, I began to run. I could hear the crowd ahead laughing, and the music was blaring, but there was no sign of my father or mother. I was lost and very frightened. Then I felt a touch on my shoulder and, turning around, there was my father. I learned that night that being lost is terrible, but being found is absolutely wonderful!

Sometimes people lose their way spiritually as well. They get out-of-touch with God, estranged from the church, and even alienated from family and friends. Jesus once told three simple stories about what it is like to be lost and then found. The first story was about a lost sheep who carelessly wandered off from the rest of the flock. The little lamb in the story did not intend to get lost, but it was enjoying nibbling away on some green grass and, when it looked up, the rest of the flock was nowhere to be seen. The same thing can happen in our relationship with God. We never intend to wander off, but days go by without saying our prayers; we get busy with other things and, before we know it, God seems very far away.

Tragically, some people do not even know they are lost until they are found. The security force in a large shopping mall found a little boy who was lost. They took him to their office and paged his parents over the intercom. While they waited, one of the officers gave the boy a big ice cream cone to eat. He was all smiles until his parents arrived, and then he burst into tears. One of the security men said, "I guess that little fellow didn't even know he was lost until he was found!" Like the lost sheep in Jesus' story, we can so easily become lost when we let other things get in the way of our relationship with God.

Jesus told a second story, this one about a lost coin and a woman who had to sweep her whole house to find it. Sometimes people get lost because others are careless or lead them astray. The coin in Jesus' story did not lose itself. It was the woman of the house who had lost the coin. Sometimes we forget how much our behavior and our attitude influence those around us. At any moment our tone of voice, our mood, or the look on our face can either draw people to Jesus Christ or turn them away from God altogether. There's an old story about a little boy who did not want to go to Sunday School. His mother said, "But, son, your father always went to Sunday School as a boy." The little boy looked up and said, "That's what I mean, Mom, it won't do me any good either!"

Then Jesus told a third story, this time about a lost son. All of us remember this story about a headstrong son who demanded his share of the inheritance, and then went off to the far country until he had wasted everything. But the point of all three of these stories is not being lost, but the joy that takes place when the lost is found. God is like the shepherd who searches for the lost lamb; God is like the woman who cleans her house to find the coin; and God is like the father who welcomes home his wayward son.

A priest was summoned for a woman dying from AIDS. "I am lost," she said, "I have ruined my life, and now I am going to hell." The priest noticed a picture on the woman's dresser. The woman said, "That is my daughter, the one beautiful thing in my life." The priest asked, "If your daughter had made a mess of her life, would you still love her?" "Of course!" said the woman. "How can you ask such a question?" "Because," said the priest, "God has a picture of you on his dresser, and God loves you just as much!"

**Benediction**

To God be the glory, both now and forevermore.

112

# 35. Draw Near To God (Lent)

**Greeting and Call To Worship**
*Draw near to God, and God will draw near to you. This is the day which the Lord has made; let us rejoice and be glad in it!*

**Opening Prayer**
O God, we long to hear your voice speaking to us, and yearn to feel your presence with us. In these moments of worship and praise, draw near to us in the power of your Living Spirit. Forgive us when we have allowed the voices of this world to drown out your voice in our hearts. Assure us now that you are with us always as we pray in the name and for the sake of Christ our Lord. Amen.

**Lord's Prayer**

**Special Hymn**                                        "In The Garden"
The writer of this much-loved hymn was C. Austin Miles. In March of 1912, he sat down in his home and opened his Bible to the twentieth chapter of John's Gospel and the story of Mary Magdalene's encounter on Easter with the Risen Christ in the garden where he was buried. He said, "As I read that story, I seemed to be a part of the scene. I became a silent witness to that dramatic moment in Mary's life, when she knelt before her Lord, and cried, 'Rabboni!' Under the inspiration of this vision, I wrote as quickly as the words could be formed in my mind, and that same evening I wrote the music." Perhaps more than any other, this hymn reminds us of God's presence with us when we submit our hearts to the Living Christ.

**Scripture Reading**                                    James 4:1-10

**Meditation**

An older couple was driving down the highway in their car one Sunday afternoon. He was behind the wheel, and she was leaning against the door on the passenger side. They were eager to get to their destination, but the car ahead of them was in no hurry at all! In it were a young man who was driving, and a young woman who was cuddled next to the driver. Occasionally, she would rest her head on the man's shoulder, and then reach up and give him a kiss. The older woman in the rear car took all this in, and then she said to her husband, "Why don't we sit together like that anymore?" Quick as a flash the husband replied, "I haven't moved!"

Now that story probably stimulates many thoughts in our minds, but the fact is, human relationships do grow cold and distant. Most of us can think of someone with whom we were very close but now we hardly communicate at all. The same thing often happens in our relationship with the Living God. We lose our enthusiasm for prayer. God seems far away. We feel out of touch, and the radiance and vitality we once had in our faith are missing. That is exactly the condition that James is speaking to when he writes, "Draw near to God, and God will draw near to you."

James knew that when our relationship with God has grown cold and distant, the problem is that we have let other loyalties and other desires get in the way. You and I are what we desire with a passion. Martin Luther once wrote: "Whatever your heart clings to and relies on is your God!" So if God seems far away, we need to ask ourselves what it is that has replaced God at the center of our lives? Is it concern over money or self or family? Is it a resentment against someone who hurt us long ago? Is it something we feel guilty about, and fear that God cannot forgive us?

Whatever has gotten in the way of our relationship with God, James' grace-filled promise is that if we draw near to God, God will surely draw near to us! He even tells us how to draw near to God: "Submit yourselves therefore to God ... Resist the devil, cleanse your hands, and purify your hearts." Now the problem for most of us is that word "submit." No matter what our age, it is hard to surrender our stubborn wills to the Lordship of Jesus Christ. Erma Bombeck in one of her books says, "Never go to a doctor whose office plants have died!" A lot of us are still trying to live life on our own terms instead of God's. We still want to trust doctors whose office plants are deader than a doornail rather than submit our wills to the Lord of all life.

In a hotel in Norway there was a little girl who loved to play the piano in the lobby, but she knew only one song and she did not play it very well. In fact, the guests were upset with her for waking them up each morning with her terrible music. Then a famous pianist spent a night in the hotel. He, too, was awakened by the terrible sounds of the piano and the little girl's attempt to make music. So he put on his robe and went downstairs to where the child was playing. He said, "I know that song. May I play it along with you?" Together they began to play, but this time the music was so lovely everyone in the hotel gathered to hear it. The difference was that the master pianist was in control! Is it too much to think that the music of our lives might take on a new lilt and luster if we gave our hearts to the Master?

**Closing Prayer and Benediction**

O God, take our hearts, our minds, and our bodies as we submit them to the Lordship of your Son, Jesus the Christ. To your name be all glory and praise both now and forevermore. Amen.

# 36. The Three Crosses Of Calvary (Holy Week)

**Greeting and Call To Worship**
*I will lift my eyes to the hills. From whence does my help come?*
*My help comes from the Lord, who made heaven and earth!*

**Opening Prayer**
O God, we stand before the Cross of Jesus Christ, unable to comprehend fully the depth of your love for sinners. We know ourselves to be people who have missed the mark, people who have sinned and come short of the glory of God. In your mercy, forgive us. In your love, help us to become in Christ the people you intended for us to be. We pray in Jesus' name. Amen.

**Lord's Prayer**

**Special Hymn**          "When I Survey The Wondrous Cross"
Isaac Watts contended that hymns should express the Christian faith in the same way that the Psalms of the Bible expressed Hebrew faith. When a teenage Isaac complained to his father about the dull and monotonous way the Psalms were sung in his time, the father became angry and said, "Well, young man, if you are smarter than King David, why don't you try to write something better?" Young Watts accepted the challenge and wrote a hymn that was sung at the service the following Sunday evening. It met with such favorable response that he continued to write hymns every week. Eventually Watts wrote more than 600 hymns, but many feel that this hymn, which captures the sorrow of Christ and the depth of God's love, is perhaps the greatest of all the hymns he wrote.

**Scripture Reading**                          Luke 23:32-43

## Meditation

When we think of Calvary, most of our attention is focused on the Cross of Jesus Christ, and that is certainly as it should be. But the attitudes of the two men who were crucified along with Jesus that day illustrate rather vividly the responses people still make to God's saving act in Jesus Christ.

One of those who hung beside our Lord symbolizes the response of rejection. You can almost hear him say, "Hey, you on the middle cross, why don't you at least yell back at those who are putting us to death? If you really are the Messiah we have waited for, then why don't you do something to save us and yourself?" But to this man, Jesus says not one word! For his question to Jesus is not really a question. It is a demand from a proud and defiant man who is unwilling to trust in anyone except himself. Because he is so focused on himself, he rejects the one person in all the world who can bring him wholeness and salvation. Perhaps you recall the famous poem by World War I Chaplain G. A. Studdart-Kennedy:

> *When Jesus came to Golgotha, they hanged him on a*
> *tree...*
> *They drove great nails through hands and feet, and*
> *made a Calvary.*
> *They crowned him with a crown of thorns, red were his*
> *wounds and deep,*
> *For those were crude and cruel days ... and human flesh*
> *was cheap.*
> *When Jesus came to Birmingham, they simply passed*
> *him by.*
> *They never hurt a hair of Him ... they only let him die.*
> *For people had grown more tender, and they would*
> *not give him pain.*
> *They only just passed down the street, and left Him in*
> *the rain.*

Like that first thief next to Jesus, we can still respond to God's gift of grace and salvation by rejection.

117

How different was the response of that other criminal to the one who was dying on the cross in the middle between the thieves! This man had nothing to offer Jesus. His past life had been one of plunder and debauchery. His future was very limited, with death coming in a matter of hours. Yet he turns to Jesus and, recognizing that this One beside him is no ordinary man, offers a simple and yet profound prayer of repentance: "Lord, remember me when you come into your Kingdom."

The forgiveness Jesus gave to that dying thief is the very same grace that God offers even now to every liar, every cheat, every failure, and every broken wreck of a human being. Sometimes we feel it was unfair that this thief received the very same grace that those who try to live saintly lives on earth have received. But the wonder of God's grace is expressed in a simple poem that we must never forget:

> *I dreamt death came the other night, and heaven's gate*
> *   swung wide.*
> *With kindly grace, an angel ushered me inside.*
> *And there to my astonishment stood folk I had known*
> *   on earth.*
> *Some I'd judged and labeled as "unfit" or "of little*
> *   worth."*
> *Indignant words rose to my lips, but never were set*
> *   free.*
> *For every face showed stunned surprise ... no one ex-*
> *   pected me!*

## Closing Prayer

God of grace, we respond in repentance to Christ, our Savior and Lord, to whom be glory forever and ever. Amen.

# 37. We Too Can Be Resurrected! (Easter)

**Greeting and Call To Worship**
*Alleluia! The Lord is risen! Let us praise the name of the Lord! Let us worship the Living God!*

**Opening Prayer**
God of power and might, we gather to praise you for the victory of the Risen Christ over sin and death. Forgive our doubting hearts and, instead, fill us with resurrection power. May the joy and gladness of Easter lift us above our darkness and distress, and may our eyes be wide open to the beauty and glory of life eternal in your Kingdom. We pray in the name of the Risen and Living Christ. Amen.

**Lord's Prayer**

**Special Hymn**                    "Christ The Lord Is Risen Today!"
We owe this wonderful Easter hymn to Charles Wesley, who first published it in 1739 with the heading, "Hymn For Easter." The music for this hymn was composed by Robert Williams, who was born in North Wales. He was born blind and trained as a basket weaver. But he was an able singer and composer with the ability to transcribe a tune after hearing it once. Together, the triumphant words and glorious tune of this hymn capture the wonder and the glory of God's Easter Victory.

**Scripture Reading**                                      John 20:11-18

**Meditation**
There is an old story about a group of confirmands being examined by the church elders before becoming members of the

119

church. The first young man was asked, "Who is the patriarch Abraham?" After a moment's thought, the boy said, "Wasn't he the first President of the United States who won the Revolution, and freed all the slaves?" There was a deep groan of frustration among the church officers. Hoping for a better answer, they asked another student, "What happened on Good Friday?" Eagerly, the young student said, "That's when Jesus died on the Cross ... and they buried him in a tomb, and rolled a stone in front of the door ... and on the third day, the stone is rolled away and he comes out ... and if he sees his shadow, he goes back in and there are six more weeks of winter!"

Those confirmation students obviously needed a little more training! But for many people, Easter is little more than an event buried in the long ago and far away. It fits in the category of fairy tale or myth, while for many others, the whole idea of someone's coming back to life after three days in the grave raises more questions that most of us care to admit. But a careful reading of the Easter scriptures reveals that resurrection was not just something that happened to Jesus — resurrection was a personal experience that happened to his followers as well! Christ arose and exploded out of the tomb, but in a very real sense his followers arose as well from their spiritual and emotional graves! Resurrection for them was not just an event in Jesus' life they lived through — it was something powerful that happened to them!

Look at what happened to people on that first Easter. Let's begin with Mary Magdalene, who came trudging to the tomb that Easter morning weeping and filled with despair. She was broken-hearted over the loss of a friend she dearly loved. Who of us here has not known what it is to walk through the valley of grief? There is no more universal experience than death, and for those who remain it is devastating and painful. Comedian George Burns wrote a book before he died about *How To Live To Be 100*. In it he has a chapter titled, "Stay Away From Funerals, Especially Your Own." We all wish we could, but the fact is we know how Mary must have felt on that first Easter.

But, suddenly, everything changes for Mary! She came looking for a dead body, but instead she meets the Risen Lord! Suddenly,

Mary experiences a resurrection! There is no more sighing or weeping in despair. Instead, she is filled with an amazing joy and rushes to tell the others, "I have seen the Lord!" We rejoice on Easter because we believe the same power of God that raised Mary from grief and despair can raise us up in our times of loss and pain.

Or recall those two travelers on the road to the village of Emmaus on Easter evening. They have not heard the news of Jesus' resurrection and, as they walk along, they are the picture of disillusionment and defeat. Again, who of us in our lives has not known that kind of disillusionment and disappointment? We put our trust in someone who has let us down. We set our hearts on a goal that suddenly becomes impossible. Hopeless and heartbroken, those two travelers to Emmaus symbolize the sense of defeat we all have known.

But, again, that is not the end of the story! While they are gripped with despair, Jesus comes and walks beside them. That night, as he breaks the bread at the table, their eyes are opened and they recognize that the same Lord they knew in this life is with them for all time! Suddenly they know there is no grave deep enough and no evil power strong enough to defeat the Living God! So let us rejoice today not only in Christ's resurrection, but in the wonderful assurance that we too can be resurrected to new life!

**Closing Prayer and Benediction**
May the power that brought Jesus from the dead fill us with new life. The Lord is Risen! He is Risen Indeed! Alleluia! Amen.

# 38. On Hoisting A Sail (Pentecost)

**Greeting and Call To Worship**

*The Lord is in God's holy temple; let all the earth keep silence before the Lord!*

**Opening Prayer**

We gather to celebrate the gift of your Living Presence with us through the power of the Holy Spirit. Come as wind, O God, and blow fresh power into our lives. Come as fire, O God, and burn away all that is destructive and sinful. Fill us with your Spirit, that we may live each day for Jesus Christ, our Lord. Amen.

**Lord's Prayer**

**Special Hymn**                                        "Holy, Holy, Holy!"

Reginald Heber, the writer of this well-known hymn, was a boyhood friend of Sir Walter Scott. He was a pastor for sixteen years in a tiny village, and it was during this pastorate that he wrote 57 hymns. "Holy, Holy, Holy" was written as a hymn of adoration and praise to the triune God. It is based on words found in Revelation 4:8, and Alfred Lord Tennyson called it the world's greatest hymn. Reginald Heber eventually became a missionary to India, but his life was cut short by a stroke and he died at the age of 43. However, most of the hymns that Heber wrote are still being sung today.

**Scripture Reading**                                            Acts 2:1-13

**Meditation**

Nothing seems so difficult for modern Christians to grasp as an understanding of the Holy Spirit. Yet nothing about our faith is more important! Because we live in a world where things are known by being seen or touched, the whole idea of the Living Presence of

God with us at each moment is very hard to understand. A teacher working with a class of 6-year-olds was trying to tell them that Jesus is always with us. She asked the class, "How do we know Jesus is with us?" One little boy said proudly, "It's Jesus who opens the door at the supermarket!"

Let's take another look at the importance of "wind" in the Pentecost story we just read. There are three words that describe the work of God's Spirit in our lives. The first is the word "intimate." The Holy Spirit is like having God's Presence in every beat of your heart, in every impulse of your spirit, in every thought of your mind, and in every motion of your will. The Hebrew word for "spirit" also means "breath." Just as a human being needs air to breathe, so a Christian needs the Spirit of Jesus living intimately in his or her heart to walk in the way of Christ.

A second word that describes the Holy Spirit is the word "intractable." What that word means is that God's Spirit cannot be tamed, domesticated, predicted, or in any way brought under human control. The same Hebrew word for "spirit" also can be translated "wind." Jesus once said, "The wind blows where it wills and you hear the sound of it...." The Holy Spirit of God is like a powerful wind — sometimes it comes as a gentle refreshing breeze into our lives and at other times it has the power of a tornado. As a sailor, I am very familiar with how quickly the wind can change direction. A friend brought me a saying that goes like this: "Sailing is hours of pure pleasure interrupted by moments of sheer panic."

The third word that describes the work of the Spirit is "inspiration." Anyone who writes poems or stories or even sermons knows what it is to be moved by the Spirit. Singers, painters, athletes, musicians, all experience that wondrous sense when the power of God seems to inspire us beyond the ordinary levels of human achievement.

But how do we harness the power of God's Spirit in everyday living? The disciples of Jesus were filled with the Spirit when they finally surrendered their hearts, minds, and wills to Jesus Christ. There is an old story about a boy who went sailing with his grandfather. He asked, "Grandpa, what is the wind?" The old sailor replied, "Son, I don't know much about the wind, but I do know how to hoist a sail!" We may not fully understand the Holy Spirit, but every one of us can hoist a sail and be filled with the power and the presence of God.

**Closing Prayer**

O God, pour out your Holy Spirit upon us. Make us one family in Christ Jesus. Encourage us with hope, and inspire us to love those around us as we let your life-giving Spirit fill our lives. We pray in Jesus' name. Amen.

**Benediction**

May the blessing of God, Father, Son, and Holy Spirit, be with you and remain with you, both this day and always. Amen.

# 39. One Nation Under God (National Holiday)

**Greeting and Call To Worship**

*If my people, which are called by my name, shall humble them-selves, and seek my face, and turn from their wicked ways, then will I hear from heaven, and will forgive their sin, and will heal their land!*

**Opening Prayer**

We give thanks, O God, for this land and for the freedom for which so many of our citizens have given their lives. We pray that the people of this nation will never forget how blessed we have been, and how important it is to trust in you as we face the uncertain future. May our leaders and our citizens remember that we are "one nation under God." We pray in Jesus' name. Amen.

**Lord's Prayer**

**Special Hymn**                    "O Beautiful For Spacious Skies"

On a summer day in 1893 Katharine Lee Bates, renowned author and professor of English at Wellesley College, stood on Pike's Peak in Colorado. On three sides of her — north, west, and south — stretched the majestic Rocky Mountains dressed in their purple haze. To the east was the fruitful Colorado plain, and just beyond were the amber-colored grain fields of Kansas and Nebraska. As she stood on the windy mountaintop, Miss Bates imagined she could see the settlers who had trekked across those grasslands decades earlier to find new homes and new opportunities in the West. She thought of the Pilgrims who had first come to America to find religious freedom, and she remembered gratefully those who had given their lives to preserve that freedom. She returned to her hotel, and the words of this beautiful hymn came to her mind. It is really a prayer that our citizens may be as beautiful as the landscape God has given us in this country.

**Scripture Reading**                                    Mark 12:13-17

**Meditation**
We celebrate with pride our national Day of Independence.
America is unique among the nations of this world. Born long before Plymouth Rock and Jamestown, America began as a vision of
freedom and equal opportunity for all people. That vision came
directly out of the religious ferment created in the Protestant and
Catholic Reformations of the sixteenth century.

It is interesting to learn how America got its name. In 1507,
Martin Waldseemuller, a German professor teaching in a French
college, edited a map of the world. Reading up on the discovery of
the New World, he said, "Much of this new land was explored by
Amerigo Vespucci ... I do not see what hinders us from calling this
new land 'America.' " So it was that a German professor in a French
college named this land for an Italian navigator in the service of
the King of Portugal! That's America — a land born in a vision of
freedom and equal opportunity for all.

But while we rejoice in our independence as a nation, perhaps
it is time for America to celebrate a "Day of Dependence" on Almighty God. Jesus set forth a very important principle about our
citizenship that we must never forget. He said, "Render to Caesar
the things that are Caesar's, and to God the things that are God's."
We are very conscious of our obligations to Caesar. Every April
15th, when we pay our income tax, all of us must render to Caesar
that which is Caesar's.

However, it is easy to forget that as followers of Jesus Christ
our real citizenship is in heaven. We belong to God and are dependent on God in a way that we must never forget. Those who founded
this nation knew that their vision of freedom and equal opportunity was based on a common faith in Almighty God. That's why in
the Pledge of Allegiance we say those words, "one nation under
God."

But as we enter a new century, many people believe America
has forgotten to "render unto God the things that are God's." We
enjoy the highest standard of living in the world — but also the
highest crime rate, the highest rate of divorce, and the highest rate

of suicide in the world! The secret to our country's greatness lies not just in our independence, but in a common dependence on the Living God. Jesus said that to become a citizen of his Kingdom one had to become like a child. A child is dependent on others for everything. A child grows only when it is loved by someone the child can trust and depend upon.

So let us rejoice in the blessings we enjoy as citizens of this great nation. But let us also commit our hearts and lives into the hands of the God who not only gave us the breath of life but, in Jesus Christ, has given us life eternal.

## Closing Prayer

God of grace and power, pour out your Spirit on this great land, that we may never forget our dependence upon you and our need for your grace and your help in all of our lives. In Jesus' name. Amen.

## Benediction

May God bless you and keep you. May God's face shine on you and be gracious to you. May God look upon you with favor and give you peace. Amen.

# 40. The Grace Of Gratitude (Thanksgiving)

**Greeting and Call To Worship**
*Sing for joy, O heavens, and exult, O earth; break forth, O mountains, into singing! For the Lord has comforted the people, and will have compassion on all those who suffer.*

**Opening Prayer**
Great God, we offer to you our praise and thanksgiving for the wondrous blessings in our lives. Most especially, we praise you for the gift of your Son, Jesus Christ, who brings us not only forgiveness for our sins, but also newness of life. Give us, we pray, the gift of thankful and grateful hearts for all your goodness to us. We pray in Jesus' name. Amen.

**Lord's Prayer**

**Special Hymn**                              "Now Thank We All Our God"
This is an amazing hymn when you consider the suffering of the pastor who wrote these words about giving thanks to God. Martin Rinkart became the pastor of the church in Eilenburg, Saxony, in Germany at the beginning of the Thirty Years' War in 1617. Because Eilenburg was a walled city, thousands of refugees swarmed into the city. The other two pastors in the city died and Rinkart was the only pastor available. He was sometimes called upon to bury up to forty or fifty people on some days. One year, 8,000 persons, including Rinkart's own wife, died in Eilenburg. It was in this time of suffering and personal heartbreak that Martin Rinkart was inspired to write this great hymn of thanks and praise to God. No doubt he recalled Paul's words about "giving thanks in everything."

**Scripture Reading**                                          Luke 17:11-19

## Meditation

A man whose father had been a pastor recalls his dad's announcing that he would preach one Sunday night on the subject, "The Worst Sin Of All." A larger than usual crowd gathered that night, wondering what human failure would the pastor label as the "worst sin." Would it be unbelief? Would it be adultery or blasphemy? The boy remembered his father speaking to a hushed and attentive congregation as he told them that ingratitude to God was the worst of all sins — because there is no room for God in an ungrateful heart.

The Bible would seem to agree with that pastor. Look at Adam and Eve. Was it not ingratitude that spoiled paradise for them? God had given them everything they possibly could want in the Garden of Eden, but their ungrateful hearts yearned for more. Or consider this incident recorded by Luke of the ten lepers who were victims of a disease so terrible that they were considered "the living dead." Yet, when Jesus miraculously heals them with the power of God, only ONE comes back to give thanks to Jesus for his new life!

Lest you think ingratitude is some ancient biblical sin that we moderns have overcome, let me tell you of a student at Northwestern University who was walking along the shores of Lake Michigan when he saw a crowded passenger ship founder near the shore. Seeing a woman clinging to a piece of wreckage, the young student threw off his heavy coat and plunged into the icy water to save her. He not only rescued that woman, but sixteen other people before help arrived. But do you know, not a single one of those seventeen people ever wrote, called, or bothered to express their thanks to those who risked their own lives to save them!

What is gratitude? The dictionary says that gratitude is "a feeling of thankful appreciation for blessings received." Now notice that word "feeling." Gratitude is more a motion of the heart than a notion of the mind. It's not gratitude when we try to force thankfulness out of our children by saying, "Now just look at all I have done for you." Gratitude, to be real, has to be heartfelt. There was a picture on a Thanksgiving card which showed a Pilgrim family on their way to worship. A grandmother showed the card to her grandson, saying, "Look at this. The Pilgrim children liked going to church with their parents." The grandson studied the card, and then said, "If they enjoyed it so much, why is the father carrying that great big rifle on his shoulder?"

Gratitude may seem like such a simple thing, but a word of thanks and appreciation can transform our relationships with others. Think for a moment how many friendships would have new life breathed into them by someone saying, "I really appreciate you." Or think of how a word of gratitude could lighten the load of that person who empties a bedpan for us, or assists us in getting dressed, or that relative who comes to visit us?

You see, gratitude for a Christian is the recognition that we owe everything we have and everything we are to the God who gave us not only the breath of life, but the wondrous gift of eternal life in Jesus Christ. That means that even in times of suffering and hardship we can still give thanks.

**Closing Prayer and Benediction**

Touch somebody's life with your life. Touch somebody's heart with yours. Share the gift of God's love with everyone you meet. Touch somebody's life with yours. Amen.

# Acknowledgments

The author gratefully acknowledges the assistance of the following books in discovering the background of the hymns used in these services:

1. *Handbook To The Hymnal*, edited by William Chalmers Covert and Calvin Weiss Laufer; published in 1946 by the Presbyterian Board of Christian Education, and printed by R. R. Donnelley and Sons, Chicago and Crawfordsville, Indiana.

2. *Crusader Hymns and Hymn Stories*, published by the Billy Graham Evangelistic Association in cooperation with Hope Publishing Company, Chicago, Illinois, 1966.

3.*The Presbyterian Hymnal Companion*, by LindaJo H. McKim, published by Westminster/John Knox Press in Louisville, Kentucky, 1993.

The author gratefully acknowledges the assistance of the following books in discovering appropriate illustrative material for these services:

1. *Some Things Are Too Good Not To Be True*, by James W. Moore, and published by Dimensions For Living, Nashville, Tennessee, 1994.

2. *Healing Where It Hurts*, by James W. Moore, published by Dimensions For Living, Nashville, Tennessee, 1993.